Building
E-Portfolios
Using PowerPoint

To all the students, young and not so young,
from whom the authors have learned so very much.

Building E-Portfolios Using PowerPoint
A Guide for Educators

Second Edition

Kathleen K. Montgomery
University of Scranton

David A. Wiley
University of Scranton

 SAGE Publications
Los Angeles • London • New Delhi • Singapore

b

For information:

Sage Publications, Inc.
2455 Teller Road
Thousand Oaks,
 California 91320
E-mail: order@sagepub.com

Sage Publications India Pvt. Ltd.
B 1/I 1 Mohan Cooperative
 Industrial Area
Mathura Road, New Delhi 110 044
India

Sage Publications Ltd.
1 Oliver's Yard
55 City Road
London EC1Y 1SP
United Kingdom

Sage Publications Asia-Pacific Pte. Ltd.
33 Pekin Street #02–01
Far East Square
Singapore 048763

Printed in the United States of America

Library of Congress Cataloging-in-Publication Data

Montgomery, Kathleen K.
Building e-portfolios using PowerPoint: a guide for educators /
Kathleen K. Montgomery, David A. Wiley. —2nd ed.
 p. cm.
Includes bibliographical references and index.
ISBN 978-1-4129-5675-8 (pbk.)
 1. Electronic portfolios in education. 2. Microsoft PowerPoint (Computer file).
3. Teachers—Rating of. 4. Students—Rating of. I. Wiley, David A. II. Title.

LB1029.P67M66 2008
371.26′0285—dc22   2007031746

This book is printed on acid-free paper.

08   09   10   11   12   10   9   8   7   6   5   4   3   2   1

Acquisitions Editor:	Diane McDaniel
Associate Editor:	Elise Smith
Editorial Assistant:	Ashley Plummer
Production Editor:	Astrid Virding
Copy Editor:	Gillian Dickens
Typesetter:	C & M Digitals (P) Ltd.
Proofreader:	Ellen Brink
Indexer:	Kathy Paparchontis
Cover Designer:	Edgar Abarca
Marketing Manager:	Nichole M. Angress

Contents

Preface   ix

Acknowledgments   xi

PART I: Assessment and the Use of Electronic Portfolios

Chapter 1: The Foundations for Portfolio Development   **3**

Introduction   3

Terms Used in Portfolio Development   5

The Advantages and Disadvantages of
     Portfolio Assessment   8

The Performance-Based Movement   11

Reflection: An Integral Part of Portfolio Development   13

The Power of Portfolios   14

Summary   19

Questions to Guide E-Portfolio Preparation   19

Chapter 2: Kinds of Portfolios and Their Uses   **21**

Introduction   21

Types of Portfolios   23

Planning for a Portfolio   26

Examples From Purposeful Portfolios   28

Summary   41

Questions to Guide E-Portfolio Preparation   42

Chapter 3: Using Standards in Portfolio Construction   **43**

Introduction   43

Standards for Teachers   46

Resources for Standards   56

Summary   58

Questions to Guide E-Portfolio Preparation   59

Chapter 4: Self-Assessment Through Reflection   **61**

Introduction   61
Rubrics Can Help   63
Reflection and Self-Assessment   66
Self-Assessment for Teachers   66
Self-Assessment Opportunities for Students   70
Summary   74
Questions to Guide E-Portfolio Preparation   74

Chapter 5: Presenting the Portfolio   **75**

Introduction   75
Presentation Skills   76
Additional Resources for Design Decisions   78
Presenting the Portfolio to Others   79
Presentation of Teacher Portfolios   80
Presentation of Student Portfolios   85
Professional Development Presentations   88
Summary   89
Questions to Guide E-Portfolio Preparation   89

PART II: Using PowerPoint to Author E-Portfolios

Chapter 6: Options for Electronic Portfolios   **93**

Introduction   93
Web-Based E-Portfolio Tools   94
Non–Web-Based (Local) E-Portfolio Tools   100
Selecting a Portfolio Tool   104
PowerPoint as an E-Portfolio Development Tool   106
Summary   108
Questions to Guide E-Portfolio Preparation   108

Chapter 7: PowerPoint Basics   **109**

Introduction   109
Start at the Beginning   110
Starting PowerPoint   111
Selecting a Slide Background   113
Selection of Font Type and Size   116
Selecting Slide Views to Accomplish Work   118
A Word About Copyright Law   126
Is There Fair Use?   126
Adding Clip Art to the Presentation   129
Adding Internet Images to the Presentation   130

Adding Sound to the Presentation 132
Adding Movies to a Presentation 134
Adding Internet or Document Links to the Presentation 135
Using Action Buttons 137
Showing the Presentation 138
Summary 139
Questions to Guide E-Portfolio Preparation 140

Chapter 8: Building Nonlinear PowerPoint Portfolios **141**
Introduction 141
Making PowerPoint Less Linear by Hyperlinking 144
Building a Structure for an Electronic Portfolio 147
Editing Images Using Basic Photoshop Elements
    Capabilities 149
Editing Sound 157
Editing Video 159
Summary 162
Questions to Guide E-Portfolio Preparation 163

Chapter 9: Tools You Can Use **165**
Introduction 165
Collecting Documents for the Portfolio 166
Of Dots and Pixels: Image Sizes 168
Scanning Materials for Use as Artifacts 170
Using Digital Cameras to Capture Images 172
A Few Photography Hints 173
Capturing and Using Digital Video 175
Saving a Portfolio to Media 178
Burning a CD 179
Saving Information to a DVD 183
Summary 184
Questions to Guide E-Portfolio Preparation 185

Chapter 10: Special Considerations and Options **187**
Introduction 187
Planning an E-Portfolio 188
What Happened? A Guide to Common
    Technical Errors 191
Downloading Required Programs—for Free 194
Downloading QuickTime—for Free 195
The Top 10 List 197
Moving a PowerPoint Presentation to the Web 198

The Future: What Promises to Make Electronic Portfolios
    More Effective?   202
Summary   204
Questions to Guide E-Portfolio Preparation   205

**Appendix: Troubleshooting Your
    PowerPoint-Based E-Portfolio**   **207**

References   **209**

Index   **213**

About the Authors   **225**

Preface

This is a book for really good teachers at all levels of instruction who wish to create electronic portfolios for their own use as a tool for self-assessment and/or for employment purposes. It is a book that cuts through the mustard of both portfolio and technology jargon. The focus is narrowed to performance, standards-based portfolios, and the technology is specific so that all teachers (college professors and in-service teachers) and preservice teacher candidates can and will use technology to enhance teaching and learning. It is our view that creating a portfolio electronically is a process that the creator owns after successful completion of an e-portfolio. This ownership of e-portfolio development can then be passed on to others; the ability to *do* what one is teaching about greatly strengthens the lesson for others. Therefore, college professors who teach this process to preservice teachers are enabling preservice teachers to use the same process with their future students. Likewise, in-service teachers who develop e-portfolios for their own professional growth and development are much more likely to use e-portfolio assessment with their own students.

Electronic portfolios present a history of accomplishments that is unique for every individual. Although we are well aware of the variety of viewpoints surrounding electronic portfolio development, we have deliberately decided to write a book that simplifies the technology part for teachers. Teachers spend an enormous amount of time maintaining expertise in both content knowledge and pedagogy. Although technology knowledge is essential for all teachers, becoming an expert in technology is not a realistic goal for most teachers. Rather, teachers do need to have the skill to use technology as a tool to augment instruction and assessment. E-portfolios can be prepared in many formats, and although this may be a good thing, it can also be daunting to teachers. Taking all of this into serious consideration, we decided to write about using PowerPoint as an e-portfolio construction tool. Our reasons are as follows:

- PowerPoint allows teachers and students to construct a presentation for which they have ownership. Unlike many turnkey options already available, PowerPoint allows individuals to choose their own background and slide construction. The skills involved in using PowerPoint are not only easy to learn but also serve to strengthen the individual's background in the appropriate technological use of fonts, color, and other design elements.

- The use of PowerPoint reduces the potential for difficulty with security issues involved in the use of the Internet or local networks. Security continues to be a problem on the Web, and the possibility of unauthorized access to e-portfolios can produce issues of privacy, liability, and intellectual property that are easily avoided through the use of presentation software. If teachers do not feel that security is an issue for them or their students and wish to have a Web-based product, then mounting a PowerPoint project to a Web site is an easy task.

❖ STUDENT RESOURCE CD-ROM

A Student Resource CD-Rom, which includes sample PowerPoint e-portfolios, is also included with the Building E-Portfolios Using PowerPoint text. The portfolio pieces that are found on the CD are tied closely to those portfolios discussed throughout the book. When you see a CD icon in the text margins, that means that there is additional material on the Student Resource CD-Rom which correlates with the book.

We hope that the ease with which the book presents information on electronic portfolios will encourage all learners to begin the journey toward self-reflective, empowered learning.

Acknowledgments

O ur reviewers provided us with thorough and relevant suggestions for strengthening each chapter of this text, and to them we are very grateful. The reviewers included Margaret Ferrara, University of Nevada at Reno; Kent Freeland, Morehead State University; D. John McIntyre, Southern Illinois University Carbondale; Amany Saleh, Arkansas State University; and Marsha Zenanko, Jacksonville State University.

We would also like to thank Diane McDaniel and Elise Smith at Sage for their expert skills throughout all stages of the publication process of this text. We thoroughly appreciate the professionalism shown by everyone at Sage and thank all of you for your very competent assistance at every step.

PART I

Assessment and the Use of Electronic Portfolios

1

The Foundations for Portfolio Development

Focus Questions

- What is a portfolio?
- How did the performance-based movement influence portfolio use?
- Why is reflection such a critical component of portfolios?
- What are the advantages and disadvantages of portfolio use?

❖ INTRODUCTION

A portfolio is a purposeful and selective collection of work showing reflection and progress or achievement over time (Montgomery, 2001). Portfolios allow for the possibility of assessing some of the more complex aspects of learning constructs, rather than just the ones that are easiest to measure. Constructivism, a major learning theory, is an approach to teaching and learning based on the premise that cognition (learning) is the result of "mental construction." In other words, students learn by fitting new information together with what they already know. Reflection on both what is known and how that relates to new work or performance can create new learning. Analyzing something as complex as teaching and learning is a prime example of constructivist theory at work. Portfolios have been used for many purposes in a variety of fields for a very long time. Traditionally, portfolios are used to show the actual work produced by individuals. People in the visual arts regularly create portfolios of their work to demonstrate their knowledge, skills, and accomplishments. Writers in all areas of writing collect examples of their best work and reflect on why these choices are regarded as "best." Any lifelong learners in any field, to demonstrate competence in any area, can use a portfolio. Those in education—teachers or students—can reap the benefits of creating a portfolio, not the least of which is identifying existing strengths and planning new short-term and long-term goals. An additional key benefit includes empowerment over one's learning. A critical component of reflection is self-assessment that focuses on the critical aspects of the learning that is taking place, thus assisting the learner to suggest modifications to future work.

The electronic portfolio, in particular, provides the author of the portfolio with a chance to present accomplishments and reflections on his or her progress in a dynamic, multimedia format. Helen Barrett (2000) offers the following advantages of electronic portfolios over traditional portfolios:

- makes evidence of work/performance more accessible, portable, and more widely distributable;
- makes performance replayable and reviewable; and
- addresses storage issues.

Portfolio construction is an authentic activity based on the application of knowledge and skills. The contents of the portfolio reveal authentic tasks or achievements that closely resemble, or actually are representative of, the challenges and standards of real life. Students, teachers, and anyone who wishes to document what they know and are able to do it within a specific context can use authentic tasks. Teachers, for example, might wish to demonstrate competency toward their ability to actively engage students in learning by presenting a video clip of a guided discovery science lesson with a voiceover explanation of the rationale for the activity. An elementary student may choose to demonstrate the ability to organize data into easily readable forms by modeling the work of a meteorologist and presenting a graph of a month's worth of precipitation for his or her town or city. High school students, working on a writing unit, may show their ability to write persuasively by including a video of an advertising commercial they wrote and directed. Preservice teachers may select a series of lesson plans as artifacts to provide evidence that they have mastered the skill of planning for differentiated instruction and a video clip to demonstrate successful implementation of the lessons. The possibility for authentic tasks that can be included in portfolios is limited only by one's imagination. The possibilities become limited, however, by the choice of a delivery system; traditional portfolios simply cannot provide the same dynamic view of the complex teaching and learning act as electronic portfolios. For example, lesson plans augmented by a video clip of students engaged in the lesson with an audio overview of students reviewing their work present the reader/viewer with a comprehensive view not offered by the traditional portfolio.

❖ TERMS USED IN PORTFOLIO DEVELOPMENT

In the literature on portfolio development and in the practice of education, new terminology has been coined or old words have been used in new ways. Multiple terms for similar, and sometimes identical, educational ideas can be confusing to practitioners who wish to create a portfolio. If those in education are operating from a common language, much of the mystery and trepidation concerning the "right" ways to define and use portfolios will disappear. For example, some authors have differentiated between student or teacher assessment and evaluation by saying that *assessment* is based on a decision about whether the student or teacher has achieved the criteria for the objective, whereas *evaluation* carries an implication of a judgment reached after assessing multiple forms of data (Eby, 1997). The two terms are often used interchangeably throughout the literature and in the schools. However, *evaluation* implies an estimate of overall value, whereas *assessment* implies a specific measure. Educators must perform both processes. Educators assess during the collection of achievement data and evaluate when determining the meaning or significance of the body of data collected. For example, assessment occurs during the artifact collection stage of portfolio development, and evaluation occurs during the final stages of reflection and goal setting. Portfolio assessment provides students or teachers with a chance to self-assess their progress toward given standards; in addition, the intended viewers of the portfolio are provided with a holistic look at the competencies of the portfolio writer. Given below is a list of terms and working definitions that Part I of this book will use to discuss the issues surrounding portfolio development:

Artifacts: An artifact is "tangible evidence that indicates the attainment of knowledge and skills and the ability to apply understandings to complex tasks" (Campbell, Melenyzer, Nettles, & Wyman, 2000, p. 147). Artifacts are the evidences or concrete representations of learning. *Portfolio documents, entries,* and *materials* are examples of terms often used interchangeably that refer to artifacts. Examples of artifacts include lesson or unit plans, photographs, video clips of students engaged in active learning, and any other evidence that indicates a standard of teaching or learning has been met.

Assessment: The term *assessment* refers to the systematic gathering of information about component parts of the thing to be evaluated.

Authentic assessment: Rather than measuring discrete, isolated skills, authentic assessment emphasizes the application and use of knowledge. Authentic assessment includes the holistic performance of meaningful, complex tasks in challenging environments that involve contextualized problems. Authentic tasks are often multidimensional and require higher levels of cognitive thinking such as problem solving and critical thinking (Montgomery, 2001).

Authentic task: This is a real-life activity, performance, or challenge that mirrors those faced by experts in the particular field; it is complex and multidimensional and requires higher levels of cognitive thinking such as problem solving and critical thinking.

E-portfolio: The electronic portfolio is a multimedia portfolio approach that allows the creator to present teaching, learning, and reflective artifacts in a variety of media formats (audio, graphics, video, and text). E-portfolios are sometimes referred to as *e-folios, electronic portfolios, digital portfolios,* or *multimedia folios.*

Evaluation: The evaluation process is broader than assessment and involves examining information about many components of the thing being evaluated and making judgments about its worth or effectiveness.

Exit portfolio: An exit portfolio is a performance-based assessment completed by the end of a teacher candidate's education program. It is a collection of artifacts and reflections that provides evidence of what the teacher candidate knows and is able to do as a result of academic and field preparation throughout the education program.

Metacognition: Metacognition is the self-appraisal and self-regulation process used in learning, thinking, reasoning, and problem solving. It is knowledge and awareness of one's own cognitive processes and how they function.

Performance assessment: This is a method of assessing learning at the understanding level, in which students produce products or performances that require demonstration of deep learning or application of knowledge. Performance assessment provides a much richer and more complete picture of what students and teachers know and are able to do.

Performance-based learning: Performance-based learning involves determining what important learning we want students to accomplish and then structuring instruction and assessment to focus on the learning based on competency, productivity, and performance standards.

Performance standards: These are shared views within the education community of what constitutes learning. Performance standards can range from unit standards selected by a teacher for use with children in a classroom setting to the standards by the Interstate New Teacher Assessment and Support Consortium (INTASC), which are often used for the initial certification of teachers.

Portfolio assessment: This includes a selective collection of work and self-assessment that is used to show progress and/or achievements over time with regard to specific criteria. A portfolio becomes portfolio assessment when the assessment purpose is defined, criteria for portfolio contents are determined, and criteria for assessing the collection of work are identified and used to make judgments about performance.

Reflection: The act of reflecting is giving careful thought, especially to the process of reconsidering previous actions, events, or decisions. Successful reflection enables self-awareness, personal and professional growth, and improved teaching practices.

Rubric: A rubric is an assessment device that uses clearly specified evaluation criteria and proficiency levels that measure achievements. The criteria provide descriptions of each proficiency level of performance in terms of what learners are able to do. (See examples of rubrics in Chapter 4.)

Self-assessment: Self-assessment asks a student to step back from a work product or process, reflect on the approach taken, analyze what went well and why, and suggest modifications to be used in subsequent performance.

❖ THE ADVANTAGES AND DISADVANTAGES OF PORTFOLIO ASSESSMENT

One of the biggest concerns about the use of portfolio assessment is that it is a great deal of work. Teaching itself *is* a great deal of work in large part because it is a process continuously in change, and change often means work. Other professions have similar concerns. For example, a surgeon must constantly study the newest, research-based surgical techniques so that patients can have the best available care. This necessitates additional study and supervised practice on the part of the surgeon. It is no different in the teaching profession. Teachers must continuously study and practice new research-based ideas in education if students are going to succeed in today's world. At the same time, change can be daunting for some teachers. It is not surprising, then, that the disadvantages of portfolio assessment tend to be teacher centered and that the advantages tend to be student centered. Again, it must be remembered that high-stakes assessment practices present a set of disadvantages all their own, not the least of which is money and time to administer and score portfolios on a large scale. The advantages and disadvantages here refer to teachers and learners at all levels outside of high-stakes, large-scale practices.

Advantages of Portfolio Assessment

- Portfolio assessment is readily integrated with instruction.
- The process of portfolio development fosters self-assessment skills and not just content knowledge.
- Reflection and goal setting help to encourage taking responsibility for one's own learning.
- The use of portfolios helps to communicate learning goals and standards to audiences beyond the student and teacher, whether it is parents, hiring boards, or one's peers.
- Portfolio use allows authors to demonstrate their thinking and learning and not just their ability to reproduce isolated facts or knowledge.

- The use of technology to enhance portfolios is a hands-on incentive for learning the technology skills needed in today's world.
- Insightful use of portfolio artifacts validates evaluations. Portfolio artifacts provide insight into the process and progress of learning, both on an individual level for the specific student and also for the teacher in a collective sense.

The benefits of portfolio use seem to outweigh the disadvantages. Teachers at all levels who are using portfolio assessment in their classrooms experience a shift in emphasis from the pencil-and-paper types of assessment to the enhancement of student performance through evaluative feedback and reflection. The process of portfolio creation fosters reflection as portfolio authors use explicit standards for judging the quality of their work. Collaboration is common as teachers and students revisit their work during peer review opportunities and revise their work as they move toward completion of the portfolio. As such, portfolios are credible vehicles of reflection, self-assessment, and communication.

Disadvantages of Portfolio Assessment

- Teachers must plan for long-term instruction that includes authentic tasks, rubrics, and self-assessment tools.
- Portfolios are time-consuming for students to assemble.
- Portfolios are time-consuming for teachers to guide and provide feedback.
- Unfocused instruction and/or ill-defined tasks lead to low reliability for evaluations in portfolio assessment.
- E-portfolios require a level of technological skill that not all teachers and students possess.
- E-portfolios require a level of technical support that not all schools are prepared to offer.

The time-consuming factors for both teachers and students may be lessened once teachers and students become familiar with the portfolio process. In addition, the use of portfolio assessment should not be looked upon as "extra" work for the teachers and students but as a different way of teaching and learning. New teaching practices tease out the older ones until the new practices are firmly in place. Requiring any innovative practice, including the e-portfolio, also requires a process of adoption that occurs over time with high levels of concern being replaced by more constructive work. Nonetheless, it is good advice to start small, perhaps with one classroom portfolio during the first year and build on portfolio use in subsequent years.

Reliability refers to the consistency and accuracy of the assessment tool to measure the desired performance. The key to developing a reliable portfolio is to establish clear and detailed criteria for success. Criteria are statements of exactly what skill or knowledge the specified groups of learners is to master, what constitutes mastery, and how progress toward mastery is measured. Criteria provide the framework for planning instruction and evaluation and, as such, should be fair, clear, and consistently applied. Criteria for both the portfolio and the contents of the portfolio should be established before students begin their work to ensure that students understand what is expected of them. Careful, periodic review of the criteria for success should take place throughout the portfolio process. In much the same way, good content validity is established in portfolio assessment. Content validity is the connection between portfolio standards and assessment criteria. If the purpose of the portfolio is in line with portfolio content standards, and clear criteria are established in relation to the standards, then the portfolio will have appropriate content validity. In general, portfolios have high content validity when instruction and assessment are in alignment because student work is directly related to the content in artifacts that are being assessed within the portfolio. Although the disadvantages of portfolio assessment are to be taken seriously, they are not so daunting that they cannot be overcome by careful planning and a willingness to embrace change.

Well-planned collaboration at all levels can be encouraging, exciting, and energy producing to learners. Perhaps the initial attempts at portfolio use should be shaped so that the experience is pleasurable and successful. Nothing breeds future success like success in the present. Teachers and students who engage in electronic portfolio development are making a promising investment in themselves.

This book explains what e-portfolios are, their purpose and contents, and how to create them using technology. There is no intent to downplay the role of standardized assessment. Portfolio assessment and standardized testing need not be mutually exclusive; both can provide important information to teachers and students. Large-scale, high-stakes standardized tests do gather information about individual student performance, but most of these assessments are primarily designed to inform decision makers about performance on the school, district, or state level. On the other hand, alternative assessment strategies are more frequently used to provide information about and for individuals. Standardized test results and quantitative data can easily be included in a portfolio and should be included if it serves the predetermined purpose of the portfolio. For example, an elementary student creating a portfolio that demonstrates progress in language arts may wish to include the scores on spelling tests in addition to writing samples. A preservice teacher might include a certificate from the Educational Testing Service (ETS) recognizing a Praxis score in the top 15% from the nationally based teacher competency Praxis exams, whereas a university professor creating a portfolio as a part of the tenure process could include a statistical analysis of student ratings over time. The key consideration in portfolio contents is to ascertain which artifacts satisfy the purpose of the portfolio. The purposes and contents of portfolios are presented in Chapter 2.

❖ THE PERFORMANCE-BASED MOVEMENT

As early as the 1970s, the United States experienced a demand for accountability in educational endeavors. State legislators, departments of education, and school districts wanted a way to know that students were learning in our nation's schools. In 1983, when the National Commission on Excellence in Education released the report, *A Nation at Risk*, educators, policy makers, and American citizens in general were dismayed and alarmed to read the following:

> The educational foundations of our society are presently being eroded by a rising tide of mediocrity that threatens our very future as a nation and a people. . . . We have, in effect, been committing an act of unthinking, unilateral educational disarmament. (p. 5)

During the years that followed this startling pronouncement, several changes have been made regarding curriculum and instruction, and these changes directly relate to today's learning theory research. The learning theory research suggests that all learning requires that the learner think and actively construct conceptual learning (Flavell, 1985). Dewey (1916) was a proponent of active learning when he wrote that knowledge and ideas emerge only from a situation (occurring in a social context) in which learners have to draw ideas out of experiences that have meaning and importance to them. Piaget (1973) demonstrated that understanding is built up step by step through active involvement, in which learners must discover relationships and ideas in classroom situations that interest them. Bruner (1966) agrees that learning is an active process in which learners construct new ideas or concepts based on their current and past knowledge.

Effective teaching research, much of which is based on the tenets of the constructivism approach to learning theory, adds that the teacher's primary responsibility is to plan and implement instruction that will involve learners in higher level thinking. According to Grabe and Grabe (1998), constructivist learning experiences and appropriate teaching and learning practices include reflective thinking and productivity along with authentic activities, peer collaboration, and consideration of multiple perspectives. Students and teachers are now being asked to demonstrate, in a significant way, what they know and are able to do. Rather than measuring discrete, isolated skills, portfolio assessment emphasizes the application and use of knowledge. The essence of performance-based portfolios is that they ask students and teachers to create something of meaning. A quality portfolio evidences complex thinking and problem solving and invokes authentic applications that represent significant learning.

A shift in thinking about learning as a teacher-directed, information-giving experience to a student-centered, performance-based approach began to emerge in education. It became necessary to replace the typically used scope and sequence charts that presented learning in a linear fashion with frameworks or standards that contain general statements of principles that allow some flexibility in what is taught and when it is to be learned (Hein & Price, 1994). This movement has extended to teacher evaluation as well. New performance-based assessment systems are being developed that require an array of reflective, analytic skills for beginning and veteran teachers. Creation of the National Board for Professional Teaching Standards (NBPTS) in 1987 resulted in the development of performance-based assessments to recognize advanced competence among experienced teachers.

The INTASC has developed a set of model performance-based licensing standards for new teachers that are compatible with the NBPTS certification standards. Combined efforts of the NBPTS and INTASC have resulted in the development of a coherent continuum of teacher development throughout the career. The INTASC has created a set of core standards that define the knowledge, dispositions, and performances essential for all beginning teachers. Further presentation and discussion on NBPTS and INTASC standards can be found in Chapter 3.

❖ REFLECTION: AN INTEGRAL PART OF PORTFOLIO DEVELOPMENT

Why are reflection and self-assessment methods such critical components of portfolios? Referring to teaching portfolios, Lyons (1998, p. 256) defines *reflection* as "a drawing together of long strands of connections, the weaving together of experiences, theories, and practices into meaning for the individual teacher and a kind of construction of knowledge—a knowledge of teaching practice." John Dewey (1933) speaks to the powerful outcomes of reflective thinking when he writes,

> We all acknowledge, in words at least, that ability to think is highly important; it is regarded as the distinguishing power that marks man from the lower animals. But since our ordinary notions of how and why thinking is important are vague, it is worthwhile to state explicitly the values possessed by reflective thought. In the first place, it emancipates us from merely impulsive and merely routine activity. Put in positive terms, thinking enables us to direct our activities with foresight and to plan according to ends-in-view, or to come into command of what is now distant and lacking. By putting the consequences of ways and lines of action before the mind, it enables us to know what we are about when we act. It converts action that is merely appetitive, blind and impulsive into intelligent action. (p. 24)

Intelligent action, as an outcome of reflection, serves to empower students and teachers to make intentional decisions as they work.

Reflective practice can also lead to monitoring and adjusting works in progress. Donald Schön (1987) describes reflective practice as a professional activity in which the practitioners reflect both *in action* and *on action* to improve their practice. When applied to teaching, this means that the teacher both experiments with these actions while they are being carried out and evaluates them by verbalizing or writing about them afterwards. Collaborative selection of portfolio contents fosters the use of metacognitive strategies recommended by cognitive development researchers. There is much agreement in cognitive research that suggests that it is extremely important to create situations in which teachers and students think about their own thinking—reflect on the ways in which they learn and why they may fail to learn (Flavell, 1985; Sternberg, 1986). As a result of such reflection, authors revise and modify their work and take the initiative to assess their own progress.

Knowledge is actively constructed by the learner, not passively received from the environment. Acceptance of new learning is a process of adaptation based on and constantly modified by a learner's experience of the world. Teachers should engage in reflective thinking about their beliefs, based on the theory that such reflection has potential to galvanize belief change (Warburton, & Torff, 2005). A major goal of authentic and portfolio assessment is to help students and teachers develop the capacity to evaluate their own work against standards that evolved from shared views within the education community of what constitutes learning (Darling-Hammond, Ancess, & Falk, 1995). Chapter 4 provides examples for methods of reflection and self-assessment.

When an electronic portfolio is used, the process of evaluating one's own work is assisted by multimedia capabilities. For example, instead of only including a hardcopy of a lesson plan in a portfolio, teachers can provide the reviewers with an edited video clip (with a voiceover explanation) of the actual implementation of the plan. In this way, reviewers can "be there" to see the effects of the plan on student learning. Students who are creating a portfolio on their skills as inventors can enrich their own learning by evaluating "live interviews" of judges' comments on the inventions submitted by students at an invention convention. The focus on the selection and evaluation of portfolio contents in both of these examples is enhanced by the use of a multimedia environment. Both the creators of the portfolios and the reviewers benefit from such a holistic, complete approach such as this.

Portfolios provide learners with an opportunity to carefully consider one's success in meeting the standards put before them, whether they are INTASC standards or standards established by a classroom teacher for the successful completion of a unit of study by a fifth-grade student. According to Martin-Kniep (1997), authors of portfolios must have a role in selecting contents, criteria for selecting work for inclusion in the portfolio must be present, and there should be some evidence of reflection in the portfolio. Having criteria for the contents of a portfolio enables the authors to focus on the process of learning to make modifications to their work before submitting a final product.

❖ THE POWER OF PORTFOLIOS

Learning is acquiring knowledge or developing the ability to perform new behaviors. Learning continues throughout our lives and affects almost everything we do. Learning can be a formal process involving teachers and schooling, and it can come from a variety of informal sources as the learner experiences the wider world. Regardless of the learning theory to which one subscribes, there is general agreement that the learning process is enhanced by knowing how to learn. Being a passive recipient of factual information without reflecting or acting on what is being learned is very limiting and, one could argue, hobbles the learner in moving forward. Consider the following all-too-familiar scenarios. Although many serious educational issues are encompassed in these scenarios, an underlying fundamental problem is that all of these teachers and learners were not given the opportunity to connect or interact with their learning environment in a meaningful way.

SCENARIO

Marcus is a primary-level student who, as a result of a phonics-driven reading program, can decode words very well. He is always called on by the teacher to read aloud and has all As in reading on his report card. Yet he never reads for pleasure and, as reported by his mother, does not seem to understand or enjoy anything that he is reading.

How a Portfolio Could Help. Using portfolios in literacy assessment allows teachers to expand the classroom horizon and enlarge each child's canvas. If Marcus's teacher were encouraged and assisted by a reading specialist and principal to use a literature-based portfolio, the teacher's instruction would necessarily need to include interesting, meaningful examination of literature relevant to Marcus and the other children in the class. Students' attitudes and motivation toward literate behaviors, such as daily literacy encounters, are taken into account for this kind of assessment. In early childhood education, portfolios should contain a clear statement of purpose and a wide variety of work samples. For a literature-based portfolio that has the purpose of assessing and documenting Marcus's attitudes toward reading, one could include samples such as Marcus's writings, drawings, logs of books read by or to him, videos or photographs of large projects, and/or tape recordings of Marcus reading or dictating stories. Marcus could select items for his portfolio based on his work on the literature he liked or found interesting.

The use of portfolios to assess young children also provides the teacher with a built-in system for conferring with parents. Rather than discuss Marcus's reading attitudes and progress in the abstract, the parents, teachers, and Marcus can review portfolio contents and celebrate specific successes. This process of feeling engaged in his learning will have the effect of increasing Marcus's desire to read for pleasure.

SCENARIO

Rebekah is a high school student who has always been curious about how things work and is looking forward to taking physics in her junior year. She is given a huge, diagram-laden textbook accompanied by many hours of classroom lecture. The teacher even has a Web site filled with more text and diagrams. The student has figured out that the contents of the Web site match the exam questions and, as a result of memorizing the information on the Web site, gets all As on her tests and an A in the course. Her parents were surprised when she decided to consider any major but those in the sciences or mathematics for her college education.

How a Portfolio Could Help. Physics is about concepts and real events around us. Quality learning and the spirit of the practice of scientific inquiry are lost when the evidence and argument for angular momentum are replaced by direct assertions from the teacher and the text. The traditional lecture demonstration method all too often yields fragmentation of student knowledge, student passivity, and the persistence of naive or even misconstrued beliefs about the physical world. Rebekah would become far more engaged in her learning if the teacher would design a portfolio around a clear-cut instructional goal, or standard, that the teacher believes all students of physics should attain. For example, a coherent instructional standard may be "to engage students in understanding the physical world by constructing and using scientific models to describe, explain, predict, and control physical phenomena." Constructing a portfolio around this clear purpose would change the instructional approach used by the teacher. A variety of labs could be planned that involve students in "understanding" the standard. Students then complete the labs and reflect on which of the labs to include in their portfolios to demonstrate that they could actually use scientific models to describe, explain, predict, and control physical phenomena. Photographs, drawings, lab reports, and science logs with students' reflections on the targeted physics concepts could all be valuable components of the physics portfolio. Rebekah's interest in mathematics and science might possibly be maintained if such an approach were taken.

SCENARIO

Alexis is a preservice elementary school teacher who has completed all of her education courses and student teaching and has prepared for a mock interview session at the college career office on her campus. After the introductions were completed and the videotape was rolling, the interviewer asked, "As a result of all you have learned and the experiences you have had to date, what do you think is the toughest aspect of teaching today?" Upon reviewing the videotape, the preservice teacher noticed a significant pause on her part before asking the interviewer, "Could you please clarify what you mean by that?" followed by an exchange that resulted in the interviewer offering several of her own ideas on the toughest aspects of teaching. Afterwards, the preservice teacher confided to the career office counselor that she knew how to teach but just could not explain it very well.

How a Portfolio Could Help. A standard that should be a part of all teacher education programs should be one that asks students to become reflective practitioners. It is not enough to be taught strategies and implement them if a preservice teacher is not given the opportunities to reflect on if and why they work. Alexis should deliberately and continuously practice reflection throughout her studies, from introductory courses to upper-level field courses. Teacher education instructors should assist their students in the development of a working portfolio that includes a focus on the reflective abilities of the students. Sample contents for the standard on reflection could include reflective essays, reaction papers, and videotapes of lessons accompanied by an analysis of the success of the lessons as well as suggested modifications for future similar lessons. As Alexis reviews her reflective work, it should be evident that a great deal of progress has been made toward refining her views of educational issues. A review of the carefully selected artifacts prior to the mock interview would assist Alexis in clearly articulating her point of view on the toughest aspects of education today.

SCENARIO

Mr. Herlihy, a public school teacher in his fifth year of teaching social studies to middle school students, knows that his lecture/recitation approach with his students does not foster the problem-solving direction that the school board wants district teachers to take. He talks with the principal about his dilemma of needing time to "cover the material" while spending additional time on problem-solving pedagogy. The principal says that she understands the problem and that the school board may take another direction after the upcoming school board elections. Later, in the teachers' lounge, Mr. Herlihy says that he is just going to wait out the school board and continue to cover the material so his students can pass the state tests.

How a Portfolio Could Help. The ongoing professional development of teachers can be greatly enhanced by the use of a teacher's portfolio. In this case, the specific focus of the portfolio should center on teachers' successful use of problem solving in their classrooms. Teachers should collect artifacts to demonstrate their use of problem-solving strategies, reflect on their teaching and its outcomes, and present their portfolios to peers. The principal could and should facilitate this process by providing the time and the means for teachers to create portfolios. This can be accomplished by designating the regularly scheduled in-service days throughout the school year as the time for teachers to develop problem-solving portfolios. Celebrating achievements is often overlooked in busy schools and would do much toward both increasing the knowledge base of teachers and creating a culture of collaboration. Mr. Herlihy would have more confidence and motivation in planning problem-solving lessons in his classroom if support for creating a portfolio were present in his school.

The use of a portfolio in each of these scenarios would provide the system that helps to align standards, instruction, and assessment. Specific, clear-cut standards help the teachers to focus on and plan for meaningful learning that is performance based. Authentic tasks in the portfolios help students to become more aware of the world around them, encourage them to think about how new ideas and experiences relate to what the students already know, and invite them to take increasing responsibility for their own conclusions and actions. The opportunity for reflection on what they are learning yields deeper understanding of the targeted concepts; the portfolio then becomes the catalyst for change and growth in both the teacher and the student.

SUMMARY

This chapter focused on the underpinnings of portfolio development, particularly the constructivist approach to teaching and learning, the role of reflection and self-assessment in portfolio construction, and the performance-based, authentic assessment movement. The case for using e-portfolios as a dynamic multimedia environment supporting constructivist theory as a replacement for the traditional paper-and-pencil portfolios was established. Chapter 2 will look at the types of portfolios and their purposes.

QUESTIONS TO GUIDE E-PORTFOLIO PREPARATION

1. What is authentic assessment and how does the definition correlate with the development of the e-portfolio?

2. How does the use of e-portfolios address what the authors actually know and are able to do?

3. What is the role of reflection in the professional growth and development of teachers and students?

4. Explain how two advantages and how two disadvantages of developing e-portfolios might affect the requirements placed on candidates by a teacher preparation program.

2

Kinds of Portfolios
and Their Uses

Focus Questions

- What kinds of portfolios are there?
- Which kind of portfolio should I use?
- Can the portfolio process be used at any level?
- What kinds of things can be a part of a portfolio?

❖ INTRODUCTION

An educational portfolio is a purposeful collection of student or teacher work that exhibits efforts and achievements. The collection must include the author's participation in selecting the contents, the criteria for selection, the criteria for judging merit, and evidence of reflection on the contents. As stated in Chapter 1, portfolio assessment not only offers an authentic demonstration of accomplishments, but it also allows students and teachers to take responsibility for the work they have done. As students and teachers reflect on their work and make goals for continued improvements, they become empowered learners. Therefore, a portfolio is a portfolio if there is a clear-cut purpose, specific evaluation criteria, negotiable contents, and elements of reflection and self-assessment. The contents are a critical selection of artifacts that depict one's knowledge and performance.

The complete definition of a portfolio must be considered when reading the literature on portfolio development. For example, many articles refer to a working portfolio. A working portfolio is a compilation of a person's work over a period of time. Technically, it probably falls in a difficult-to-define category similar to that of trying to determine the biological category in which a virus belongs. Many authors see the working portfolio as just a collection of work over time because it lacks the critical portfolio attributes of self-assessment and criteria for content selection. These authors agree that, as such, the working portfolio is not a true portfolio. For example, a teacher's working portfolio could include lesson plans, units, and all forms of teacher-prepared materials over a career. It can contain works in progress as well as finished samples of work. One could use the working portfolio to document growth toward performance standards as it includes materials that provide evidence of accomplishments at various benchmarks. Granted, it is an intentional collection of work, but its use is limited to being a receptacle for work unless the use of the contents is clear-cut and defined from the beginning. The value of a working portfolio is in having a ready source of pertinent work from which to choose the contents for any kind of portfolio that has a specific purpose.

The purpose of the portfolio—its focus or intended use—is far more important than the name that researchers give to describe a particular portfolio. Purposes can include evaluating learning progress, applying for college or employment, or certifying new and master teachers, to name a few. Both the purpose and the audience for the portfolio need to be clearly established so that the author can focus on meaningful organization of the portfolio contents. It is also important to note that when teachers understand the portfolio process, they also understand that it can be applied at all levels, from the primary grades to the graduate level. Later in this chapter, examples of proficiency portfolios for use by in-service teachers, preservice teachers, college professors, and educators in general will be presented.

❖ TYPES OF PORTFOLIOS

There are many different names given to types of portfolios, which can be confusing to those who are thinking of creating them. Although the types of portfolios can be distinct in theory, they tend to overlap in practice. It is less important to correctly "name" the portfolio than it is to decide on a specific focus or purpose of the portfolio. Two major types of portfolios with distinct purposes are the academic portfolio and the professional portfolio. An *academic portfolio* is an organized record of academic experiences, achievements, and professional development over a period of time. It consists of a collection of documents that illustrates the variety and quality of work completed, along with reflections on these documents. It is a record of academic career events that provides evidence for the development of teaching service and research quality. Trigwell, Martin, and Benjamin (2000) suggest that an academic portfolio provides the author with the means to develop a personal philosophy of teaching and research and, through reflective discussion about academic achievements, provides the impetus to take action on future achievements that is both informed and planned. As such, an academic portfolio can inform the rank and tenure process and can also serve as an employment tool. *Professional portfolios* allow educators to display their best work in a way that sets those educators apart from the crowd. A portfolio can be used to give evidence of many skills and abilities that administrators desire in a teaching candidate. Portfolios provide a venue to demonstrate reflective thinking strategies, show professional growth over time in diverse educational situations, and relay personal attitudes toward teaching and learning. The portfolio serves as proof of the accomplishments achieved during teaching experiences or educational careers. By selectively collecting work and personal documents of achievement, educators can build a visual representation of their past contributions that allow others to gain a deeper and clearer picture of where they have been, where they are now, and where they are going in the education profession.

To lessen the confusion for the beginning portfolio author, we will use two basic types of portfolios selected because they each have a specific purpose. Therefore, progress-oriented portfolios and product-oriented proficiency portfolios will be discussed. The academic portfolio can serve the purpose of showing the proficiency of the author regarding academic achievement. The professional portfolio can also serve the purpose of showing progress in learning or proficiency in accomplishments. In addition, the progress-oriented professional portfolio can evolve into a proficiency portfolio. For example, a preservice teacher can create a progress-oriented professional portfolio that reflects on and documents growth in the process of designing lesson and unit plans. Goals for continuing improvement can be made. As the preservice teacher reaches proficiency in planning skills, a product-oriented professional proficiency portfolio can then develop. The following chart explains the alternate names and purposes for these portfolios:

Progress-Oriented Portfolio

Purpose: To document the processes of learning and to give evidence for improvement in knowledge and performance in any given area
   Alternate names:

- Progress portfolio
- Developmental portfolio
- Process portfolio
- Professional portfolio (with the purpose of showing progress)

Product-Oriented Proficiency Portfolio

Purpose: To provide evidence of competence and accomplishments in a specific area
   Alternate names:

- Best work portfolio
- Presentation portfolio
- Showcase portfolio
- Display portfolio
- Exit portfolio
- Interview portfolio
- Professional portfolio
- Teaching portfolio
- Academic portfolio

Considering the following more specific information on each of these types of portfolios will assist the teacher in deciding which kind suits the teacher's purpose:

Progress-oriented portfolios: These portfolios tell the story about the growth of teachers. They document the processes of learning, including earlier drafts, reflections on the process, and challenges encountered along the way. The following describes possibilities for work samples (artifacts) that could be included in a progress portfolio from the point of view of the preservice teacher, the in-service teacher, and college instructors.

Preservice Teachers

Lesson plans written in the same content area methods course over a term, as well as reflective analyses of lessons and goals for continuing improvement

---

In-Service Teachers

Classroom management plans at the beginning, middle, and end of a school year; reflective statement on the efficacy of the plans and suggested modifications; and evidence that school standards for appropriate classroom management have been met by the end of the school year

---

College Instructors

A statistical graph over three terms depicting the results of student evaluations of an instructor in the same course, evidence that the scores and written feedback on student evaluations have been considered, specific modifications that have been made to enhance the scores, and a written plan for continuing improvement

---

When selecting artifacts, or content, for the progress-oriented portfolio, it is important to remember that like samples should be compared to determine progress. For example, a lesson plan should be compared to a previous lesson plan; an essay should be compared to a previous essay and not just any piece of writing. Reflection on the learning process is a key component of the progress portfolio, as well as establishing present and future goals for continuing improvement.

Proficiency portfolios: These portfolios serve to demonstrate an individual's best work, a showcase of exemplary documents and accomplishments in any given area. The contents can represent a subset of materials from a working portfolio. The following chart describes artifacts that might be included in a proficiency portfolio:

Preservice Teachers

Reflective statements on exit standards from an education program, as well as artifacts of all kinds that demonstrate knowledge and performance, which demonstrate proficiency toward meeting those standards

In-Service Teachers

Plans for a series of teacher-to-teacher workshops conducted by a teacher, evaluations of those workshops, reflection on the evaluative feedback, and a reflective statement on the benefits of planning and conducting workshops for colleagues

College Instructors

Statement of why one believes that tenure is deserved, list of presentations and publications, a record of service to the college and the community, and evidence of successful teaching practices

A proficiency portfolio can document a teacher's best work accomplished during a unit, field experiences, undergraduate school, or an entire career. The proficiency portfolio details accomplishments in a specific area and can demonstrate readiness to receive a specific proficiency designation such as graduation, certification, or readiness for employment. The proficiency portfolio provides its audience with substantial evidence of levels of mastery related to performance standards and goals. Regardless of the kind of portfolio selected, the portfolio provides the means to continuously examine new skills as a result of intelligent reflection on existing performance at all levels of learning.

❖ PLANNING FOR A PORTFOLIO

Beginners to portfolio development find that it is hard work, but the professional growth and development that occur as a result of this introspective process are very rewarding. Peter Seldin (1997) explores why portfolio use, especially the teaching portfolio, has had a slow start among teachers at all levels and why it is such a necessity to use one:

Swelling pressure from such diverse sources as the Carnegie Foundation for the Advancement of Teaching, the American

Association for Higher Education, state legislatures, faculty, and students have moved institutions to reconsider the importance of teaching and the role of the teacher in the classroom. Countless institutions are reexamining their commitment to teaching and exploring ways to improve and reward it. Some teachers even regard teaching as so straightforward that it requires no special training. Others find it so personal and idiosyncratic that no training could ever meet its multiplicity of demands. But most share the common folk belief that teachers are born and not made. In fact, the marginal truth in this belief applies no more to teaching than to any other profession. If there are born teachers, there are born physicians, born attorneys, and born engineers. Yet those who are naturally great at these professions invariably spend an unnatural amount of time acquiring skills and practicing in the vortex of intense competition. (p. 4)

The professional growth that comes from constructing a portfolio is worth the time spent in gathering evidence of one's competency and reflecting on the larger picture of one's accomplishments. Presenting the portfolio to others allows teachers at all levels to communicate both what they know and are able to do. As more and more teachers use portfolios, they increasingly recognize that the process has the power to transform teaching and learning.

Part II of this book clearly describes how to construct an electronic portfolio and how a multimedia approach can provide a rich description of knowledge and performance. Although planning for a hard-copy portfolio does not differ in principle from planning for an electronic portfolio, one should keep in mind that electronic artifacts can be linked to each other and across standards, as the writer feels appropriate. Following these basic guidelines will help to keep the author centered on the final outcome:

- Establish a clear-cut purpose that is linked to criteria standards and has a specific audience in mind. For example, a best-work (proficiency) portfolio for a beginning teacher looking for employment could be centered on the standards from the Interstate New Teacher Assessment and Support Consortium (INTASC). INTASC is a consortium of state agencies, higher education institutions, and national educational organizations dedicated to the reform of the education, licensing, and ongoing professional development of teachers. The audience could be an interviewing team composed of teachers, administrators, and parents.

• Select artifacts that provide evidence that the standards have been met. Artifacts should be directly related to the purpose and organized thoughtfully. Introductions, explanations, and reflections should accompany all artifacts.

It is important for portfolio authors to be clear about their goals, to focus on the reasons they are engaging in a portfolio project, and to keep in mind the intended audience for the portfolio. The purpose of the portfolio needs to be carefully considered as it drives all decisions in the portfolio process.

❖ EXAMPLES FROM PURPOSEFUL PORTFOLIOS

In this section, representations of the portfolio process for teachers in higher education, as well as preservice and in-service teachers, will be presented. Suggestions for content and ways in which the electronic multimedia format can enhance the portfolio will be discussed.

Proficiency Portfolios for Teachers

Proficiency-teaching portfolios encourage personal professional development and improvement as well as document evidence for personnel decisions. The following list suggests possible contents for a teaching portfolio for teachers through the university level:

Statement of teaching philosophy	Résumé or vitae
Teaching evaluations	Classroom observations by others
Special skills or knowledge	Lesson plans
Student work samples and teacher evaluations of those samples	Reflective analyses of teaching and professional development plans
Classroom management plans	Course syllabi
Assessment rubrics used	Unit plans
Teacher-created materials and projects	Scholarly publications and presentations

Videotapes of lessons, interviews	Photographs
Examples of interaction with students and/or parents	Service and volunteer activities
Motivational techniques and analyses of success	Examples of technology use
Awards and certificates earned	Professional documented activities

This list is, of course, not inclusive of all possible artifacts, and one should not select them all. Rather, it is meant as a "starter list" to help the author think about the range of possibilities for selecting artifacts. With electronic portfolios as well as with hardcopy portfolios, more is not necessarily better. The goal in artifact selection should be to select those artifacts that correspond with and enhance the purpose of the portfolio while, at the same time, not overwhelming the reviewers.

Refer to the INTASC portfolios on the Student Resource CD

Example From a Preservice or First-Year Teacher's Proficiency Portfolio. The following examples can be found on the CD that accompanies this book.

Example 1 INTASC Standard Five: Learning Environment: The teacher uses an understanding of individual and group motivation and behavior to create a learning environment that encourages positive social interaction, active engagement in learning, and self-motivation.

Reflection: As a professional, I have learned that being aware of the classroom dynamics is very important. Individual and group behaviors need to be observed and monitored regularly. Corrective actions need to be taken promptly to ensure positive social interaction. A teacher that understands the students' behaviors as a group can create a positive learning environment. Allowing students to actively engage in activities and discuss topics as a group are great ways to get the students motivated and excited about learning.

Artifact: I created an individual behavior contract with the "class clown" who, although truly being humorous, was distracting to others. I listed the specific behaviors of the student, presented the list to him, and asked for clarification. The student owned the behaviors and understood how distracting they were. Because they were habitual behaviors, I made a chart with the behaviors listed and asked the student to monitor the frequency

---

(Continued)

(Continued)

of the behaviors during lessons. The behaviors nearly disappeared and were clearly at a manageable level. The student self-selected a reward, which was to visit the guidance counselor and report his progress. The learning for me was invaluable; helping this student to take charge of his behavior choices helped me as a teacher focus on maintaining a healthy learning environment. As an artifact, please see the contract I created.

Example 2 **INTASC Standard Six: Communication: The teacher uses knowledge of effective verbal, nonverbal, and media communication techniques to foster active inquiry, collaboration, and supportive interaction in the classroom.**

Reflection: Standard Six means that the teacher does not simply stand in front of the class and speak throughout every lesson while the students sit and listen silently in their seats. The teacher encourages student discussions, ideas, and inquiry throughout the lesson. Effective methodology is used such as use of Internet-based Webquests, guided discovery, and cooperative learning groups to maintain an active, social learning environment that scaffolds the new information into previous learning in a meaningful way.

Artifact: The artifact I chose was the guided discovery lesson plan "Being Alive" from a Math and Science Methods course. I chose this artifact because the guided discovery strategy asks students to think critically and engage in inquiry. In this lesson, the students went out in their surroundings and discovered either a living or nonliving object and were then asked to apply what they learned in the classroom to the object. As the teacher, I planned several key questions to assist students with discovering the concepts contained in my objectives.

Example 3 **The University of Scranton Unit Exit Standards (correlated with INTASC standards): Teacher as Scholar: The teacher plans teaching models that use major concepts, principles, theories, research, and technology related to learning, including attention to diverse learners.**

Reflection: Effective teachers are capable of designing lessons that integrate curricular concepts, current educational theories and principles, and research and technology to best serve the needs of the diverse classroom population. This means that effective teachers must be able to plan lessons to ensure the learning success of all students.

Artifact: Artifact 1 is a photograph of an integrated reading and science learning center designed for primary-level students entitled "Why Does It Rain?" The center includes hands-on activities, such as an electro-board and the creation of a rain cycle mobile, as well as reading activities and a Web site activity. This artifact meets the standard because it incorporates science curriculum with student-centered learning theories. In addition, this center is designed to ensure the academic success of kinesthetic as well as auditory and visual learners.

Integral to the creation of a portfolio is the process of reflection that takes place on the author's view of achievement on the standards criteria being used. For each standard in Examples 1 to 3, preservice teachers have written an interpretive statement (reflection) that emerged from their reflective process. The artifact was then carefully selected to represent the standard, and it is paired with a relevant and insightful reflection on why it was selected. The author's teaching is being evaluated through the reflection and selection of the artifact. The preservice teacher in Example 1 makes the point that teachers need to be alert and aware of the individual and group actions of students and plan appropriate, student-centered interventions. In Example 2, the teacher clearly sees teacher communication as an active two-way process with the students. Questioning and inquiry lessons are strategies deliberately used to attain this level of communication. The preservice teacher in Example 3 views planning as an integrative process using technology and active learning strategies that strive to meet the needs of diverse learners. Additional artifacts as seen on the CD will add a stronger picture to the philosophy of teaching of these teacher candidates and present the audience with a clear and focused analysis of the candidates' capabilities as teachers.

Refer to the Student Resource CD for additional artifacts

Example From a Teaching Portfolio for Rank and Tenure in Higher Education. A teaching portfolio in higher education grows out of the conception that teaching is an integral part of academic scholarship, which also includes research and service. This type of portfolio includes work samples of teaching, research, and service, as well as reflective commentary on those samples that help to clarify their meaning within the context of one's philosophy of teaching. The purpose of the teaching portfolio for rank and tenure decisions is very clear: to establish a record of consistently successful achievements in teaching, research, and service that will satisfy the existing university standards for attaining promotion or tenure. *Consistently successful achievements,* however, should not be construed as selecting only best work or a biased picture of one's work but should be determined by the author's philosophy of teaching statement. As Zubizarreta (1994) suggests,

Even the occasional flop is worthy material for a portfolio if it reveals a process of genuine adjustment and growth, if the teacher has articulated innovation and risk as key components of a teaching philosophy, and if the institution recognizes experimentation and change as signals of vitality in teaching. (p. 325)

Where to begin, then, seems to lie in developing a clear statement of teaching philosophy by reflecting on and articulating one's values and goals in teaching. Reflection on how one's scholarship agenda and service are integrated into this teaching philosophy will help to demonstrate coherence to one's work. This process of reflection helps to define the standards for the individual and, as such, clarifies the choice of artifacts selected to provide evidence for the standards.

The following hypothetical example of a personal teaching statement from a teacher in higher education shows the connection among teaching, scholarship, and service:

Teaching Philosophy Example

The following principles of learning provide fundamental structure for me as a teacher and learner. They form a framework on which I shape my courses, scholarly work, supervision, student mentoring, service, and other faculty activities:

- Providing learners with experiential, authentic learning opportunities promotes the transfer of theoretical learning to practical learning.
- A major goal of teaching is to guide learners toward becoming contributing members of society.
- Teachers and learners must appreciate and value diversity in our world.
- Specific, timely, and meaningful feedback helps learners to reflect on and modify their academic, social, and emotional learning.
- It is the teacher's job to educate the whole person.
- Success stimulates further success.
- All teachers must seek continuous renewal and growth.

I believe that my accomplishments as a teacher indicate a steady history of incorporating these principles of learning in the areas of teaching, scholarship, and service. All artifacts in this portfolio will provide evidence that supports this teaching philosophy.

The principles of learning found in this teaching statement can be regarded as the individual standards that guide the teaching, research, and service choices made by the author. The next task becomes one of selecting artifacts that provide evidence that these standards were met. The electronic portfolio can provide a vibrant, rich picture of how this higher education instructor works toward these standards. Figure 2.1 shows how one could plan for an electronic "page" that would demonstrate attainment of the first standard concerning the author's focus on moving students from theory to practice.

Subsequent standards can be addressed in much the same way. The kind of presentation format used in the electronic portfolio helps the reader see *if* and *how* the portfolio author is "practicing what he or she preaches." It makes the complex process of teaching more apparent and more dynamic. The design process also provides the author with a chance to view these works in a way that allows the connections of professional choices to emerge. The insight derived from this process assists the higher education instructor with identifying existing strengths and formulating specific goals for continuing improvement.

Example From a Teaching Portfolio for In-Service Teachers. There is a growing consensus that a standards-based teaching portfolio is an important means of furthering the reflective practice of teachers and assessing the level of their professional performance (Hebert, 2001; Parkay & Standford, 2004). These dual outcomes for constructing a K–12 teaching portfolio are widely stated in the INTASC literature. It promotes standards-based reform through the development of model standards and assessment for beginning teachers. The INTASC standards will be more fully discussed in Chapter 3. Whether the outcome of a teaching portfolio is a more informed teacher or an award of licensure, the fact remains that teaching is a complex process that requires a complex approach to accurately measure its effectiveness.

As with all portfolios, the purpose has to be clearly defined by the individual teacher before beginning portfolio construction. Perhaps a veteran teacher wishes to obtain a National Board for Professional Teaching Standards (NBPTS) certificate. There are many reasons why a teacher would want to obtain an NBPTS certificate, some of which are described by the National Association of State Directors of Teacher Education and Certification (NASDTEC, 2000) as follows:

Figure 2.1 Example of Portfolio Design for Teaching Statement Standard on Transferring Theoretical Learning to Practical Learning

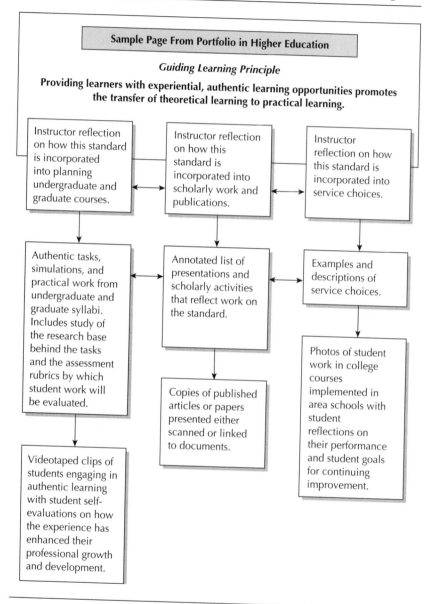

A variety of additional NBPTS financial incentives and stipulations are state-specific. Alabama makes a one-time allocation of $5,000 to her/his school when a teacher earns an NBPTS certificate. Florida

requires an NBPTS-certified teacher to earn a satisfactory annual performance evaluation as a prerequisite for receiving an annual supplement equal to 10% of the prior year's average statewide classroom teacher's salary. Such Florida teachers who provide the equivalent of 12 workdays of mentoring services are eligible for an additional 10% supplement. Massachusetts requires an NBPTS-certified teacher to mentor a new teacher in her/his school in order to earn an annual salary supplement. Kentucky advances an NBPTS-certified teacher to the Rank I salary classification. (p. 2)

The NBPTS standards become the framework, then, for veteran teachers to demonstrate what they know and are able to do as professional educators. The electronic portfolio in particular, as with the higher education portfolio, provides the teacher with the platform that can highlight the integrative aspects of teaching with authentic examples of planning and student performance. Figure 2.2 shows how multiple data sources in an electronic portfolio can provide demonstrable evidence that a standard has been met. In this case, the NBPTS standard that the teacher is addressing is "Standard XII: Collaboration with colleagues: Accomplished generalists work with colleagues to improve schools and to advance knowledge and practice in their field."

The easily accessible video clips and photos presented in an electronic portfolio are a far more effective demonstration of performance than a descriptive list of collaborative experiences often found in paper portfolios. In addition, standards are connected to one another and overlap in many ways. The linkages that can be made between and among artifacts in electronic portfolios assist the reviewers in getting a complete, robust picture of what the teacher knows and is able to do.

Classroom Portfolios Designed by Teachers for Students

Although the focus of this book is on portfolios created by educators, the authors believe that, once the process has been successfully completed by a teacher, it is a relatively easy task to use portfolio assessment with students. Therefore, the remaining section of this chapter provides the reader with the possibilities for classroom portfolios designed by teachers for their students. The function of classroom portfolios, or portfolios that students complete as a result of meeting the requirements established by a teacher, can be of any type. They can show student proficiency toward meeting instructional standards or growth in any given area. Regardless of the type of portfolio, students will have a negotiated

Figure 2.2   Possible Selection of Artifacts as Evidence That Standard XII
Has Been Met

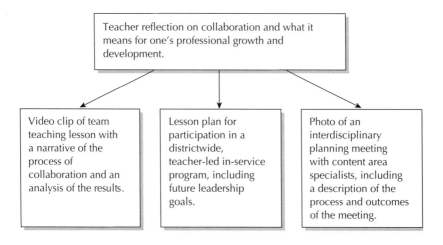

Sample Page From a Veteran Teacher's Portfolio

National Board for Professional Teaching Standards (NBPTS)

Standard XII: *Collaboration With Colleagues:* Accomplished generalists work with colleagues to improve schools and to advance knowledge and practice in their field.

Teacher reflection on collaboration and what it means for one's professional growth and development.

Video clip of team teaching lesson with a narrative of the process of collaboration and an analysis of the results.

Lesson plan for participation in a districtwide, teacher-led in-service program, including future leadership goals.

Photo of an interdisciplinary planning meeting with content area specialists, including a description of the process and outcomes of the meeting.

choice regarding the contents, and there will be opportunities and evidence for reflection and student self-assessment. The act of assembling a portfolio can be very motivating to students because it not only is an engaging activity but is also about *them* and their work. The personal aspect of the portfolio can further motivate students to produce high-quality work. The following list of possible contents of a classroom portfolio shows the scope of conceivable choices:

Statement about learning from unit	Personal statement
Journal and log entries	Photographs of projects
Writing samples	Interest inventories
Self-assessment rubric	Reflective analyses

Goals for continuing improvement	Annotated reading lists
Book talks	Maps
Murals	Designs and sketches
Posters	Models
Artwork	Lab experiments and reports
Solutions to problems	Quizzes and tests

Again, these suggestions for portfolio artifacts are not meant to be all-inclusive but rather are a limited number of possibilities from which a teacher planning a portfolio might choose. The purchase of a digital camera or two would be a good investment for taking photographs of large or three-dimensional artifacts such as murals and models.

Students and teachers will learn many technology skills throughout the process of developing a portfolio; as such, the electronic portfolio becomes an absorbing authentic technology task. The following technology skills represent a range of skills useful to electronic portfolio construction:

- Using a scanner to scan images and text documents
- Using PowerPoint to create nonlinear projects with navigation through hyperlinks
- Planning for and recording narration and reflections
- Operating digital cameras and video digital cameras
- Using drawing and formatting tools to enhance the presentation of artifacts
- Editing photos and video clips
- Creating Word documents, including brochures and other specific types of documents

Most teachers are not yet proficient in the use of these technology skills and will decide either to start small and/or use the services of the technology teachers in the school system. This type of collaboration is necessary to the success of all involved in the portfolio process. School administrators should be prepared to facilitate such collaboration and, in fact, become collaborative colleagues in supporting all attempts to implement standards-based portfolio development.

Portfolio Example for Elementary Students. This portfolio is planned by the teacher as part of an instructional unit on the "Rain Forests of the World." After selecting the standards that will become the basis for instruction, the teacher plans numerous activities and individual assessments for those activities. The teacher decides that the portfolio will be a best-work portfolio and wants the students to choose an artifact from each of five key standards in the unit. The teacher will choose the standards, and the students will select an artifact that represents their best work toward meeting each of those standards. The intended outcomes of this unit on the rain forest are derived from the standards that the teacher has selected and are as follows.

The students will do the following:

- Develop and practice skills necessary to work collaboratively with others
- Develop and use speaking and listening skills appropriate to a variety of contexts
- Decode, interpret, respond to, and critically analyze ecological positions
- Collect, analyze, and organize information
- Use cooperative means to bring research together in an organized manner
- Access appropriate data to support geographic research from computer, encyclopedia, and other resources
- Identify various plants and animals of the rain forests
- Identify and illustrate the geographic location of rain forests
- Explain why rain forests are endangered
- Explain why rain forests are necessary for planet ecology and list ways that people can help preserve the environment

Before students begin actual work on the rain forest unit, the teacher clarifies the purpose and requirements of the portfolio. Students have access to rubrics that will be used to evaluate their work and are given lessons on and opportunities for reflection and self-assessment. Students will become familiar with how to use a digital camera and scanner, and they will have lessons on how to download pictures and documents to the computer. Figure 2.3 shows how the Table of Contents page might look as developed by a student who has completed all unit work and has constructed an electronic portfolio.

The audience for the portfolio should also include peers and/or family members. The amount and quality of work that goes into portfolio assessment should culminate in a celebration of learning. In elementary school settings, portfolio parties can be planned so that students can share their work and learning with others. Another class can benefit from reviewing a peer's electronic rain forest portfolio, with the author taking the lead role in the presentation. Portfolios such as this also help parents to specifically see what their children know and are able to do and, consequently, become more aware of their children's achievements in school.

Portfolio Example for Secondary Students. Many middle school and high school students feel detached from learning and assessment experiences that are unidimensional and represent a "regurgitation" of information presented through daily lectures. Group and project work does much to get high school students more involved in their work, and the process of portfolio construction can provide secondary students with a sense of pride and accomplishment in their work efforts and products. For the secondary student to feel successful at the end of constructing a portfolio, the teacher has to carefully consider the following in planning for portfolio implementation:

- Instructional goals and performance standards for the portfolio are clearly articulated in both the minds of the teacher and the students.
- The purpose of the portfolio should be clearly explained to students.
- The instructional strategies should be aligned with the performance standards and should flow logically from the portfolio purpose.
- The selection criteria for the contents should be developed along with scoring rubrics and self-assessment forms; the students should receive this information prior to beginning work on the portfolio.
- Students should be given ample time to show that they understand the selection criteria for artifacts and all other procedural rules established by the teacher.
- Student-teacher communication should be maintained throughout the implementation of the portfolio.

Figure 2.3   Example of Content Organization for Electronic Portfolio on
the Rain Forests

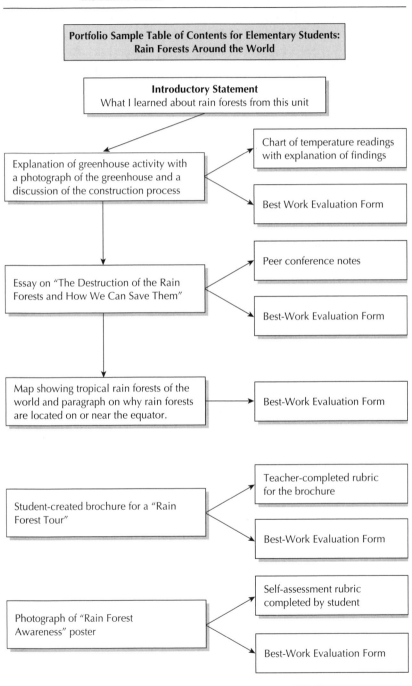

This seems like a great deal of work, and it is. One must first decide to limit lecturing to students and use daily class time for unit lessons that culminate in product or process outcomes that can become portfolio contents, or artifacts. In addition, staff development and planning opportunities need to be a part of the culture of learning in standards-based teaching and learning.

To illustrate how a classroom portfolio for a secondary student could evolve, we present part of a social studies unit on culture in Figure 2.4. For this introductory exploration of culture, the teacher has selected Theme IX from the National Council of the Social Studies Standards (NCSS): Social studies programs should include experiences that provide for the study of global connections and interdependence. The teacher has planned the unit around this theme and has included a variety of activities that introduce students to all aspects of another culture, including the beliefs, customs, practices, and social behavior of people within a culture.

The section of the electronic portfolio shown in Figure 2.4 illustrates evidence that the student can recognize the similarities and differences between his or her own culture and another culture. At the same time, the student has not only benefited from practicing authentic technology skills but can also demonstrate products of learning that show the connectedness of the student's work.

SUMMARY

The examples presented in this chapter represent only a few ways in which an electronic portfolio can take shape. As long as the purpose of the portfolio is clearly established and the artifacts provide evidence of performance toward clearly written standards, then the design of the portfolio is limited only by one's imagination. The process of creating an electronic portfolio will be a positive and energizing learning experience if careful planning and decision making occur prior to and throughout the process.

The next chapter will discuss the place of standards in portfolio development. Standards describe knowledge, performance, and skills that are important over a lifetime of learning for the quality teacher.

Figure 2.4   Sample Page From a Portfolio Entry From the Culture Unit

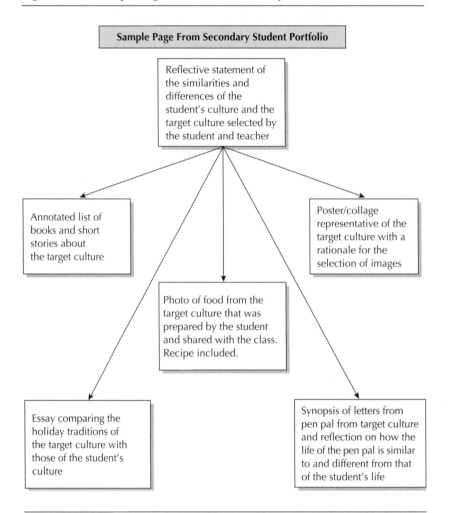

QUESTIONS TO GUIDE E-PORTFOLIO PREPARATION

1. Which type of e-portfolio is most suited for use in teacher preparation programs?

2. What can you do with an e-portfolio that might be more difficult to do in a more traditional paper-bound portfolio?

3. List at least a dozen artifacts that might be produced in both an academic and professional portfolio.

3

Using Standards in Portfolio Construction

Focus Questions

- Why are standards so important in education today?
- What standards apply to the professional growth of teachers?
- Where can I find standards?

❖ INTRODUCTION

Standards are shared views within the education community of what constitutes learning. Performance standards, in particular, require an active generation of response that is observable directly or indirectly by a permanent product or process. Performance standards also are representative of real-world, or authentic, issues or problems. Portfolio assessments derived from performance standards ask learners to create a product that demonstrates their knowledge and skills, thus providing evaluators with a rich and complete picture of what learners know and are able to do. The strongest argument for using standards is that teachers and students are all focused on what all groups should know and be able to do. Standards create common ground on which learning foundations are built. Standards are important because they serve to clarify and raise expectations and also provide a common set of expectations (Kendall & Marzano, 1996). Kendall and Marzano (2004) noted some problems, however, on the scope, purpose, and nature of standards and suggest that a systematic effort be undertaken to remedy the following areas of concern:

(1) multiple documents (137 documents across 14 areas of study were consulted) that state what students and teachers should know and be able to do—there needs to be a single comprehensive review so that states can identify information important to them;

(2) differing types of content description within these documents can cause confusion among states when selecting and understanding standards, such as

- procedural standards written as the learner is able to edit an essay,
- declarative standards written as the learner understands the conventions of punctuation,
- contextual standards written as the learner uses appropriate tone and style for a selected audience.

Although Kendall and Marzano (2004) addressed the concerns of curriculum developers in K–12, these concerns are valid for all levels of documents. However, they are by no means insurmountable concerns. Perhaps professional agreement pertaining to national standards would best resolve the issues listed above, and many professional organizations have done just that. For example, the National Council for Teachers of Mathematics (NCTM, www.nctm.org), the National Science Teachers Association (NSTA, www.nsta.com), the National Council for the Social Studies (NCSS, www.ncss.org), the National Council for Teachers of English (NCTE, www.ncte.org), and the International Technology Education Association (ITEA, www.iteaconnect.org) represent the major content-oriented national organizations that have developed quality performance-based standards, as shown in the following chart:

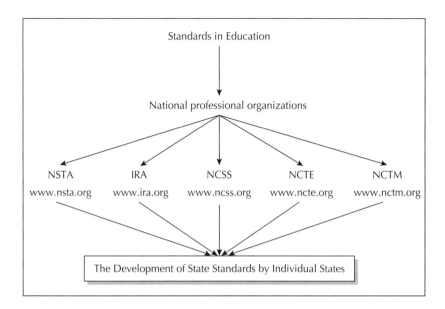

It is important to note that educational technology standards apply to all content areas at every level. Technology standards are governed by the ISTE, the International Society for Technology in Education. The ISTE has developed standards for students, teachers, and administrators and includes a profile of skills these populations should be able to perform to meet the appropriate standard.

NETS•T for Teachers
(Performance indicators for each standard can be found at
http://cnets.iste.org/teachers/t_stands.html)

ISTE National Educational Technology Standards for Teachers (NETS•T)

Standard 1: Technology Operations And Concepts

Teachers demonstrate a sound understanding of technology operations and concepts.

Standard 2: Planning And Designing Learning Environments And Experiences

(Continued)

(Continued)

Teachers plan and design effective learning environments and experiences supported by technology.

Standard 3: Teaching, Learning, And The Curriculum

Teachers implement curriculum plans that include methods and strategies for applying technology to maximize student learning.

Standard 4: Assessment And Evaluation

Teachers apply technology to facilitate a variety of effective assessment and evaluation strategies.

Standard 5: Productivity And Professional Practice

Teachers use technology to enhance their productivity and professional practice.

Standard 6: Social, Ethical, Legal, And Human Issues

Teachers understand the social, ethical, legal, and human issues surrounding the use of technology in PK–12 schools and apply those principles in practice.

The ISTE National Educational Technology Standards for Teachers (NETS•T), which focus on preservice teacher education, define the fundamental concepts, knowledge, skills, and attitudes for applying technology in educational settings. The process of portfolio development can meet many of these standards as students gain knowledge of and apply skills, such as planning for a multimedia presentation, hyperlinking, and using CD-R technology. In addition, the artifacts themselves can indicate proficiency with technology, such as a lesson plan that has technology embedded in the lesson as a natural part of instruction, evidence of the use of desktop publishing activities with students, or work with Webquests either planned for student use or created by the teacher.

❖ STANDARDS FOR TEACHERS

The purpose of a preservice teacher's portfolio is to document professional growth and development. Many teacher preparation programs are requiring education students to create an exit portfolio to demonstrate performance-based evidence that they have met the standards of the program. Standards often are derived from state agencies that regulate the certification of teachers (see list and Web addresses of state agencies on the CD), but standards can also come from national accreditation agencies such as the National Council for Accreditation of Teacher Education (NCATE). NCATE standards address the skills, knowledge, and dispositions that are expected of every teacher candidate. The NCATE standards are closely aligned with and elaborate on the 10 model standards for teacher licensure developed by the Interstate New Teacher Assessment and Support Consortium (INTASC). The INTASC standards outline a coherent continuum of teacher knowledge, skills, and dispositions for beginning teacher professional development. The point here is that, although there are state and national standards, a common language among standards is understood by professionals who review portfolios. Spending time thinking about what the standards mean to one's achievements, professional growth, and development is time well spent.

Refer to the Student Resource CD for more department of education web links

When selecting the standards and guidelines for preservice portfolio construction, many colleges and universities decide to use a combination of state and national standards because of the correlation between them. The connection among standards should be made clear to preservice teachers to assist them in taking the mystery out of interpreting multiple sets of standards.

The University of Scranton's model for the preparation of professional educators sees the preservice teacher as a scholar and decision maker (see Figure 3.1).

The model has several strands of reflective practice built in to enhance the decision-making abilities of preservice teachers. These standards are available to students as soon as they enter the education program so that students can review their work as they proceed through the program. As students reflect on their work and improve it after receiving instructor feedback, they can decide to use it as an artifact that provides evidence of having met a performance standard. Figure 3.2 extends the model for the preparation of professional educators with a final column of possible artifacts that pertain to the standards for elementary education students.

The artifacts presented are in no way intended to be an exhaustive list of what should or could be included in an electronic exit portfolio for preservice teachers. Rather, because students will be conversant

Figure 3.1 Model for the Preparation of Professional Educators, Created by Dr. Deborah Eville Lo, University of Scranton

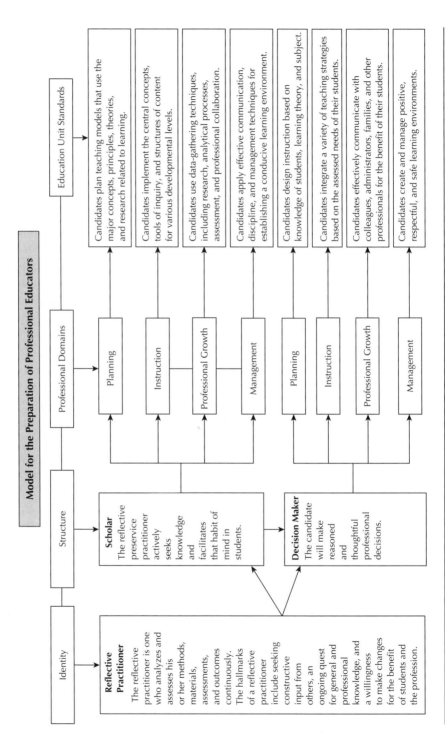

with the unit standards from the time they enter the education program, students can decide, as they progress through the program, which artifacts to use. In this way, the students can be creating a working portfolio of all standards-related achievements and then select exemplary artifacts for the exit portfolio. An exit portfolio can also provide the preservice teacher with a portfolio that will enhance the initial job search and interview process. Feedback that results from presentation of the exit portfolio can be used before molding the exit portfolio into a portfolio for employment.

In keeping with the definition of standards as shared views within the education community of what constitutes learning, the INTASC standards were developed for licensing new teachers (see Figure 3.4).

The INTASC standards were developed by representatives from the teaching profession along with personnel from 17 state education agencies. These standards were developed to be compatible with the advanced certification standards of the National Board for Professional Teaching Standards (NBPTS). This work helps to develop a coherent approach to educating and licensing teachers based on shared views among states and within the profession of what constitutes good teaching.

The NBPTS standards are presented here (see Figure 3.5) as well so that one can readily see the compatibility and overlap among standards for teachers. Although the NBPTS standards are used for veteran teachers, the differences from one set of teaching standards to another is negligible and provides more evidence that standards really are a composite view of what the profession states that teachers should know and be able to do. Many universities and state agencies have developed their own sets of standards for evaluating teacher performance, and since standards are a shared view of what is important for quality teaching and learning to occur, such standards *can* be tailored to individual institutions but can also connect to national standards.

The Education Department at the University of Scranton has designed an exit portfolio for preservice teachers based on the INTASC standards and the Pennsylvania Department of Education (PDE) standards. Figure 3.3 shows how the University of Scranton unit standards correlate with the INTASC standards for beginning teachers. For example, the more global INTASC Standard 2 is aligned with the more specific standards for both Scholar 1 and Scholar 4 in the Scranton standards. Thus, preservice teachers understand how children learn and develop, and they can provide learning opportunities that

Figure 3.2   Samples of Possible Artifacts for Education Department Unit Standards, University of Scranton

A Sampling of Artifacts for an Elementary Preservice Teacher Using the Scranton Model

Education Unit Standards	Partial Listing of Artifacts That Demonstrate Success in Meeting the Standard
Candidates plan teaching models that use the major concepts, principles, theories, and research related to learning.	Integrated, thematic lesson plans and rubrics Short-term and long-term goal statements Research papers
Candidates implement the central concepts, tools of inquiry, and structures of content for various developmental levels.	Lesson plans created for a variety of grade levels Guided-discovery lesson plan with photos or video of children working Teacher-designed tasks that give students a choice of products Content supervisor's evaluations
Candidates use data-gathering techniques, including research, analytical processes, assessment, and professional collaboration.	Anecdotal student records with reflective analysis on use Authentic tasks and rubrics that support learning standards Student journals samples and how they are used Evaluations of student work
Candidates apply effective communication, discipline, and management techniques for establishing a conducive learning environment.	Philosophy of classroom management statement Room arrangements that facilitate communication Classroom rules with rationale for the rules
Candidates design instruction based on knowledge of students, learning theory, and subjects.	Student interest inventories and prior knowledge assessments Lesson plans and units that demonstrate attention to individualized instruction strategies Photos and explanations of an integrated learning center
Candidates integrate a variety of teaching strategies based on the assessed needs of their students.	Lessons that demonstrate a variety of strategies that allow students to explore concepts in depth Reflective essay on how to access the prior knowledge of students and the impact of this knowledge on instruction Interest inventories and their use in planning instruction
Candidates effectively communicate with colleagues, administrators, families, and other professionals for the benefit of their students.	Team-planning/team-teaching experiences with reflection on process Newsletters, notes to parents, parent conference notes, and comments Portfolio review parties with other classes Field trips and guest speakers
Candidates create and manage positive, respectful, and safe learning environments.	Reflection on appropriate elementary learning environments Survey of student comments on the established learning environment Letters from parents and students Observations from others

Figure 3.3 Alignment of the University of Scranton Standards and INTASC Standards

The University of Scranton Unit Standards

As Scholars, teacher candidates . . .

1. Planning	2. Instruction	3. Management	4. Professional Growth
Plan teaching models that use major concepts, principles, theories, research, and technology related to learning, including attention to the needs of diverse learners.	Implement the central concepts, tools of inquiry, and structures of content for the various developmental levels of diverse populations and use continuous reflective self-assessment for professional growth.	Use data-gathering techniques that include research, analytical processes, assessment, and the use of appropriate technology throughout the curriculum. Candidates practice proper professional behaviors and deal ethically with colleagues, superiors, students, and families.	Apply effective verbal, written, and technological communication and management techniques, and react with sensitivity to the various needs and feelings of students, families, colleagues, and others.

As Decision Makers, teacher candidates . . .

1. Planning	2. Instruction	3. Management	4. Professional Growth
Design instruction for the diversity of student needs, based on the use of appropriate learning theory and content knowledge, including academic content standards, multicultural materials, and technological options.	Develop goals and objectives appropriate for all students and integrate a variety of teaching strategies based on the assessed needs of their diverse student population.	Show concern for peers and students by managing positive, respectful, and safe learning environments and by demonstrating the belief that all children can learn.	Effectively communicate with colleagues, administrators, families, and other professionals and facilitate the social acceptance of diverse populations by encouraging positive relationships and considering feedback from those relationships. Appropriate professional behaviors are practiced consistently.

(Continued)

Figure 3.3 (Continued)

The Teacher . . .   *Interstate New Teacher Assessment and Support Consortium (INTASC) Principles*

Understands the central concepts, tools of inquiry, and structures of the discipline he or she teaches and can create learning experiences that make these aspects of subject matter meaningful for students.	Understands how children learn and develop and can provide learning opportunities that support their intellectual, social, and personal development.	Understands how students differ in their approaches to learning and creates instructional opportunities that are adapted to diverse learners.	Understands and uses a variety of instructional strategies to encourage students' development of critical thinking, problem solving, and performance skills.	Uses an understanding of individual and group motivation and behavior to create a learning environment that encourages positive social interaction, active engagement in learning, and self-motivation.	Uses knowledge of effective verbal, nonverbal, and media communication techniques to foster active inquiry, collaboration, and supportive interaction in the classroom.	Plans instruction based on knowledge of subject matter, students, the community, and curriculum goals.	Understands and uses formal and informal assessment strategies to evaluate and ensure the continuous intellectual, social, and physical development of the learner.	Is a reflective practitioner who continually evaluates the effects of his or her choices and actions on others (students, parents, and other professionals in the learning community) and who actively seeks out opportunities to grow professionally.	Fosters relationships with school colleagues, parents, and agencies in the larger community to support students' learning and well-being.
INTASC 1 *Aligned with Scholar 1*	INTASC 2 *Aligned with Scholar 1, 4*	INTASC 3 *Aligned with Scholar 2; Decision Maker2*	INTASC 4 *Aligned with Decision Maker 1*	INTASC 5 *Aligned with Scholar 3; Decision Maker 3*	INTASC 6 *Aligned with Decision Maker 3*	INTASC 7 *Aligned with Decision Maker 1*	INTASC 8 *Aligned with Decision Maker 2*	INTASC 9 *Aligned with Scholar 4; Decision Maker 3, 4*	INTASC 10 *Aligned with Decision Maker 4*

Figure 3.4   The Interstate New Teacher Assessment and Support
Consortium (INTASC) Standards

INTASC Standards for Beginning Teachers

Standard 1: Content Pedagogy

The teacher understands the central concepts, tools of inquiry, and structures of the discipline he or she teaches and can create learning experiences that make these aspects of subject matter meaningful for students.

Standard 2: Student Development

The teacher understands how children learn and develop and can provide learning opportunities that support a child's intellectual, social, and personal development.

Standard 3: Diverse Learners

The teacher understands how students differ in their approaches to learning and creates instructional opportunities that are adapted to diverse learners.

Standard 4: Multiple Instructional Strategies

The teacher understands and uses a variety of instructional strategies to encourage student development of critical thinking, problem solving, and performance skills.

Standard 5: Motivation and Management

The teacher uses an understanding of individual and group motivation and behavior to create a learning environment that encourages positive social interaction, active engagement in learning, and self-motivation.

Standard 6: Communication and Technology

The teacher uses knowledge of effective verbal, nonverbal, and media communication techniques to foster active inquiry, collaboration, and supportive interaction in the classroom.

Standard 7: Planning

The teacher plans instruction based on knowledge of subject matter, students, the community, and curriculum goals.

Standard 8: Assessment

The teacher understands and uses formal and informal assessment strategies to evaluate and ensure the continuous intellectual, social, and physical development of the learner.

Standard 9: Reflective Practice: Professional Growth

The teacher is a reflective practitioner who continually evaluates the effects of his or her choices and actions on others (students, parents, and other professionals in the learning community) and who actively seeks out opportunities to grow professionally.

Standard 10: School and Community Involvement

The teacher fosters relationships with school colleagues, parents, and agencies in the larger community to support students' learning and well-being.

support their intellectual, social, and personal development (INTASC Standard 2) by

• planning teaching models that use major concepts, principles, theories, research, and technology related to learning, including attention to the needs of diverse learners (Scholar 1) and by

• applying effective verbal, written, and technological communication and management techniques, as well as reacting with sensitivity to the various needs and feelings of students, families, colleagues, and others (Scholar 2).

This connection is made clear to students at the very beginning of portfolio development so that the "living" component to e-portfolios can easily be maintained by changing standards as one progresses throughout one's educational career. Of course, new reflection opportunities are presented as well as the selection of new artifacts.

This alignment with the INTASC standards facilitates preservice teachers with the option to modify their e-portfolio to incorporate the INTASC standards if they so choose before interviews.

With passage of the No Child Left Behind Act of 2002 (see U.S. Department of Education, 2002), Congress reauthorized the Elementary and Secondary Education Act (ESEA), the principal federal law affecting education from kindergarten through high school. In amending the ESEA, the new No Child Left Behind Act represents a sweeping overhaul of federal efforts to support elementary and secondary education in the United States. A key component of this law is ensuring that there are "highly qualified" teachers in the nation's schools. National Board certified teachers (NBCTs) use the NBPTS to earn national certification (see www.nbpts.org). The No Child Left Behind Act recognizes NBCTs as meeting the law's requirements of being highly qualified. Given this, it is a logical assumption that more states will encourage teachers to become National Board certified, which includes portfolio assessment as a major element of earning such certification. The times are changing in American education, and standards are leading the way.

Figure 3.5 NBPTS Early Adolescence/Generalist Standards

The National Board for Professional Teaching Standards (NBPTS) Early Adolescence/Generalist Standards (for teachers of students ages 11–15) These standards serve as the basis for National Board Certification in this field.	
I. Knowledge of Young Adolescents Accomplished generalists draw on their knowledge of early adolescent development and their relationships with students to understand and foster their students' knowledge, skills, interests, aspirations, and values.	**VII. Multiple Paths to Knowledge** Accomplished generalists use a variety of approaches to help students build knowledge and strengthen understanding.
II. Knowledge of Subject Matter Accomplished generalists draw on their knowledge of subject matter to establish goals and to facilitate student learning within and across the disciplines of the middle-grades curriculum.	**VIII. Social Development** Accomplished generalists foster students' self-awareness, character, civic responsibility, and respect for diverse individuals and groups.
III. Instructional Resources Accomplished generalists select, adapt, create, and use rich and varied resources.	**IX. Assessment** Accomplished generalists employ a variety of assessment methods to obtain useful information about student learning and development, to inform instructional strategies, and to assist students in reflecting on their own progress.
IV. Learning Environment Accomplished generalists establish a caring, stimulating, inclusive, and safe community for learning where students take intellectual risks and work independently and collaboratively.	**X. Reflective Practice** Accomplished generalists regularly analyze, evaluate, and strengthen the effectiveness and quality of their practice.
V. Meaningful Learning Accomplished generalists require students to confront, explore, and understand important and challenging concepts, topics, and issues and to improve skills in purposeful ways.	**XI. Family Partnerships** Accomplished generalists work with families to achieve common goals for the education of their children.
VI. Respect for Diversity Accomplished generalists model and promote behavior appropriate in a diverse society by showing respect for and valuing all members of their learning communities and by expecting students to treat one another fairly and with dignity.	**XII. Collaboration With Colleagues** Accomplished generalists work with colleagues to improve schools and to advance knowledge and practice in their field.

❖ RESOURCES FOR STANDARDS

The following Web sites will assist all portfolio authors in selecting standards to guide portfolio development. Above and beyond simply listing the standards, each of the organizations listed below discusses the instructional and assessment practices deemed appropriate for each field of study. The rationale and background for the standards are also presented.

Science standards (http://search.nap.edu/readingroom/books/nses/html/). The *National Science Education Standards* presents a vision of a scientifically literate populace. These standards outline what students need to know, understand, and be able to do to be scientifically literate at different grade levels.

Language arts standards (www.ncte.org). This is the homepage of the National Council of Teachers of English (NCTE). A joint effort between the NCTE and the International Reading Association (IRA) yielded English-language arts standards for K–12 that define what students know and are able to do. These standards encourage the development of curriculum and instruction that make productive use of the emerging literacy abilities that children bring to school. In addition, the standards provide ample room for the innovation and creativity essential to teaching and learning.

Foreign-language standards (www.actfl.org). This is the homepage of the American Council of Teachers of Foreign Language (ACTFL). *Standards for Foreign Language Learning in the 21st Century,* which includes information applying the standards to specific languages, was released in 1999. These standards represent a consensus among educators, business leaders, government, and the community on the definition and role of foreign-language instruction in American education.

Mathematics standards (www.nctm.org). This is the homepage of the National Council of Teachers of Mathematics (NCTM). The *Principles and Standards for School Mathematics* of 2000 addresses content, teaching, and assessment. These standards are guidelines for teachers, schools, districts, states, and provinces to use in planning, implementing, and evaluating high-quality mathematics programs for kindergarten through Grade 12.

Social studies standards (www.ncss.org). This is the homepage of the National Council for the Social Studies. *Expectations of Excellence: Curriculum Standards for Social Studies* and *Standards* *for the Preparation of Social Studies Teachers* consist of 10 themes incorporating fields of study that roughly correspond with one or more relevant disciplines. These 10 themes span the educational levels from early to middle grades to high school. Student performance expectations within these themes are then specified, and examples of classroom activities are provided as illustrations of how to design learning experiences to help students meet the performance expectations.

Physical education standards (www.aahperd.org). This is the homepage of the American Alliance for Health, Physical Education, Recreation and Dance. The *Outcomes of Quality Physical Education* outlines the outcomes for physical education in kindergarten through Grade 12. Content standards and assessment material based on the outcomes document were developed and can be found at this site.

Standards for the fine arts (www.artsedge.kennedycenter .org/professional_resources/standards/nat_standards_main.html). Developed by the Consortium of National Arts Education Associations (under the guidance of the National Committee for Standards in the Arts), the *National Standards for Arts Education* is a document that outlines basic arts learning outcomes integral to the comprehensive K–12 education of every American student.

Technology standards (www.cnets.iste.org). This is the homepage of the National Education Technology Standards (NETS). *Curriculum and Content Area Standards* and the *Technology Foundation Standards for All Students* consist of categories that provide a framework for performance indicators for students learning to use technology in all content areas. Teachers can use these standards and profiles as guidelines for planning technology-based activities in which students achieve success in learning, communication, and life skills. Technology standards for teachers are also included at this site. There are many useful lesson plans that indicate how teachers can effectively use technology with students.

Standards for music education (www.menc.org). This is the homepage of the National Association for Music Education. The *National Standards for Arts Education* is a statement of what every young American should know and be able to do in four arts disciplines—dance, music, theater, and the visual arts. The scope of these standards is from kindergarten through Grade 12, and they speak to both content and achievement.

Teaching standards for beginning teachers (www.ccsso.org/ intascst.html). This is the homepage of the Council of Chief State School Officers (CCSSO). The INTASC is a project of the CCSSO. The INTASC standards represent a common core of teaching knowledge and skills that are designed to help all students acquire 21st-century knowledge and skills. The standards were developed to be compatible with the advanced certification standards of the new NBPTS. The INTASC standards address the knowledge, dispositions, and performances deemed essential for all teachers regardless of their specialty area.

Teaching standards for veteran teachers (www.nbpts.org). This is the homepage of the National Board for Professional Teaching Standards, which has developed standards in 27 fields. All NBPTS standards are based on the National Board's *Five Core Propositions* for what accomplished teachers should know and be able to do. The standards serve as the basis for National Board certification, which some states have adopted for promotion or for additional financial compensation for teachers.

Technology, innovation, design, and engineering educators (www .iteaconnect.org). This is the homepage of the International Technology Education Association. The *Technological Literacy Standards* promotes technological literacy for all students, teachers, and administrators.

SUMMARY

Standards are important in every aspect of education because they create common ground for learning at all levels. Long gone are the days when teachers did what they thought was best and hoped that it indeed was the best. Standards help to guide teachers in what their students should learn and present a framework for teachers' own professional growth and development as well. In the next chapter, the role of reflection and self-assessment in portfolios will be discussed along with the use of rubrics to guide self-assessment.

QUESTIONS TO GUIDE E-PORTFOLIO PREPARATION

1. Of what importance are standards in e-portfolio development?

2. Discuss which standards best serve your purpose in e-portfolio development. Why do you think as you do?

3. Who authored the standards you will be using in your e-portfolio? Are the NETS•T represented in these standards? If so, how?

4

Self-Assessment
Through Reflection

Focus Questions

- Why are reflection and self-assessment important in portfolio development?
- What role does a rubric play in self-assessment?
- What are some examples of reflection?
- How do reflections on standards help with the selection of artifacts?

❖ INTRODUCTION

Self-assessment asks a teacher or student to step back from a work product or process, reflect on the approach taken, analyze what went well and why, and suggest modifications to be used in subsequent performance. Ongoing self-assessment leads to learner assurance that one's abilities are approaching an expert level. One can have faith in one's abilities best through reflecting on those abilities, examining what we already know and can do, and then generating new goals for further improvement. This mental processing is what gives teachers, students, and all learners confidence in themselves. This is what leads learners to personal empowerment. Learners who practice self-reflection become aware of the misconceptions and misunderstandings they hold, and only then can a path for growth and development be determined. This holds true for very young children as well as university professors and all teachers and students in between. All learners need to go beyond describing the artifacts in their portfolios and move to analyzing and appraising the artifacts and then thinking about how this appraisal transforms their learning. When students question, examine, and evaluate their own behavior and accomplishments, they gain confidence in exercising their own judgment.

An important attribute of the successful reflective learner, both teacher and student, is the ability to focus on the ongoing efforts to understand their work better. Thus, reflective teachers will engage in classroom-based inquiry, both formal and informal. Bondy and Ross (2005) state that reflective teachers are never satisfied that they have all the answers and constantly challenge their own practices and assumptions. Such inquiry-based learning is an active learning approach focusing on questioning, critical thinking, and problem solving. Inquiry is an engaging process that often leads to new ideas and new considerations. Inquiry is the cornerstone of constructivism that is founded on the premise that, by reflecting on our experiences, we construct our own understanding of the world in which we live. Lee Shulman (1987) has identified seven broad categories of knowledge that constitute the major categories of the knowledge base for a classroom teacher that are necessary for successful, reflective teaching practice:

- Content knowledge
- General pedagogical knowledge, with special reference to those broad principles and strategies of classroom management and organization that appear to transcend subject matter
- Curriculum knowledge, with particular grasp of the materials and programs that serve as "tools of the trade" for teachers
- Pedagogical content knowledge, a teacher's own special form of professional understanding
- Knowledge of learners and their characteristics
- Knowledge of educational contexts, ranging from the workings of the group or classroom, to the governance and financing of school districts, to the character of communities and cultures

- Knowledge of educational ends, purposes, and values, as well as their philosophical and historical grounds

Arguably, this is the knowledge base that comes from successful completion of a program of education. For preservice teachers, field experiences in classrooms provide an opportunity to apply what they have learned. Thus, learning to teach becomes grounded in an authentic, real-world context. The professional growth and development of the preservice teacher can be encouraged and supported by reflective practice. The reflective process for teachers can encourage teacher interaction and collegial sharing and give them a genuine interest in their own professional development. Although some people may seem to have a natural ability to reflect and self-assess, most need assistance and practice with reflective thinking.

❖ RUBRICS CAN HELP

A rubric is defined as an assessment device that uses clearly specified evaluation criteria and proficiency levels that measure achievement of those criteria (Montgomery, 2001). The criteria provide descriptions of each level of performance (e.g., outstanding, average, poor) in terms of what students or teachers know and are able to do.

Rubrics are useful when a judgment of quality is required, and they can be used in a variety of subjects, products, and processes, including reflective activities. Learners are aware of and control their learning by actively participating in reflective thinking. This is why reflection is a critical part of portfolio assessment because once learners become aware of their learning performance and reflection on that performance occurs, the next step is evaluating the quality of learning and suggesting an improvement plan. Reflective thinking is a part of the critical thinking process of analyzing and making judgments about an action, decision, or performance. Therefore, the evaluation criteria in a rubric could be centered on analytical skills, thinking skills, and/or the ability to evaluate.

For example, suppose a teacher wanted to evaluate the teaching strategies he or she currently uses. A rubric could assist the teacher in becoming aware of the strategies being used and help the teacher to rate the effectiveness of strategies on student learning. The first step in designing a rubric for the self-assessment of lesson effectiveness is to list the evaluation criteria that comprise an effective lesson. These criteria can come from commonly used lesson evaluation tools that are based in the effective teaching research. An example of such criteria is as follows:

- Lesson activities should be congruent with lesson objectives.
- The purpose of the lesson should be communicated to students in relevant terms.
- An introduction should be planned and implemented so that students become interested in the lesson.
- The lesson should match student interests, needs, and attitudes, and there should be provisions to involve students in the lesson.
- Vocal qualities, the use of gestures, and teacher movement should all serve to enhance learning.
- Support materials should be accurate and suitable, and they should enhance understanding of the lesson.
- Effective questioning techniques should be implemented.
- Deliberate ways to formatively assess student learning should be planned and implemented.
- An appropriate closure should be planned and implemented.

The next step is to select three to five proficiency levels for rating purposes. The proficiency level that indicates the highest level of attainment should be listed first, with the lowest level in the far-right column. Once the rubric is designed, the teacher (elementary, high school, or college) could videotape a lesson and complete the rubric while viewing the lesson:

Criteria	Exceptional	Acceptable	Need Help
The lesson activities are congruent with lesson objectives. *Evidence:*			
The purpose of the lesson is communicated to students in relevant terms. *Evidence:*			
The introduction serves to get students interested in the lesson. *Evidence:*			
The lesson matches student needs, interests, and attitudes and provides for student involvement. *Evidence:*			
Voice, gestures, teacher location in the room, and body language are all used effectively. *Evidence:*			

Criteria	Exceptional	Acceptable	Need Help
Supporting materials are accurate and suitable, and they enhance understanding of the lesson. *Evidence:*			
Effective questioning techniques were implemented. *Evidence:* Deliberate ways to formatively assess student learning were implemented. *Evidence:*			
An appropriate closure was implemented. *Evidence:*			

As the teacher rates the performance, evidence for the rating should be considered and noted on the rubric. For example, if a teacher rating for "voice, gestures, teacher location in the room, and body language are all used effectively" was at the "need help" level, the evidence might look like this:

Evidence: My voice seemed very loud and rather monotone. I stayed at the front of the room with my hands in my pockets for almost the entire lesson.

This analysis can then easily turn into a plan for change that might include varying voice volume and inflection and increasing the use of gestures and movement around the room. The reflective cycle continues with additional observations and gathering of evidence to determine if improvement and progress toward goals are occurring. The criteria, the ratings, and the evidence for ratings become the basis of a plan for continuing improvement that is in alignment with effective teaching practices and the teacher's philosophy of teaching statement. As teachers determine which artifacts to include in their portfolios, they can refer to the self-assessment rubrics they have used. Reflections on why these artifacts have been selected are logical outgrowths of the critical thinking that occurred while using the self-assessment rubrics. Examples of student rubrics are presented later in this chapter. It is important to note that the learner, one's peers, or one's teachers can complete rubrics.

❖ REFLECTION AND SELF-ASSESSMENT

Reflection and self-assessment go hand in hand. The key to reflection is the skill in asking and answering probing questions about what one knows and is able to do. Reflection and self-assessment occur best in an environment that models, prompts, and supports reflective thinking. Students in PK–12 and teachers at all levels need a nonjudgmental, emotionally supportive environment that focuses on thinking and not just the accumulation of information. The process of self-assessment includes reviewing the learning situation, determining specific strengths and the evidence for that determination, and suggesting specific goals for improvement, including how those goals will be met. As learners at all levels begin to feel comfortable with self-assessment, the process continues as learners consider the worth of their own work against publicly stated standards. A significant part of this process is the ability to reflect on attitudes, skills, and ideas and to be willing to change and update these areas through continued learning.

❖ SELF-ASSESSMENT FOR TEACHERS

A teaching portfolio, whether for teachers in basic education or higher education, is an essential part of the teacher's professional growth and development. In today's climate of teacher accountability, teacher self-assessment contributes to the enhancement of teacher quality. As previously mentioned, the teaching portfolio should begin with a statement of teaching philosophy, and all of the artifacts should support this philosophy. Reflection and self-assessment are necessary for choosing the artifacts, and questions become the foundation for engaging in the reflective process. Some examples of questions that would stimulate self-assessment for teachers include the following:

- Which teaching strategies used do you believe are the most effective, and what supports your belief?
- What content area do you view as your strongest? Are there content areas in which you need to improve? What is your plan for doing so?
- How do you individualize your teaching approach to meet the needs of all students?
- Give examples of alternative teaching approaches you have used.
- How have scholarly works or presentations you have completed affected your teaching?

- What use have you made of student and peer evaluations of your teaching?
- How have your service opportunities contributed to your teaching?

A list of questions such as the above should follow and emerge from writing the teaching statement and become the catalyst for reflective thought. As teachers respond thoughtfully to a set of questions, the artifacts have a coherence that is directly related to the teaching statement. For example, the following reflections on each of the Interstate New Teacher Assessment and Support Consortium (INTASC) standards by a preservice teacher guide the selection of artifacts presented in an e-portfolio (see CD):

Refer to the INTASC portfolios on the Student Resource CD

Standard 1: Subject Matter Reflection

As a teacher, I plan to make learning activities for my students both authentic and meaningful. Effort will be made at all times to make connections between classroom activities and the lives of my students. Knowledge of subject matter is not enough: An effective teacher must understand how to make subject matter meaningful for students.

Standard 2: Student Learning Reflection

Teachers must not only understand child development and patterns of learning, but they must also be able to use that knowledge to create learning experiences that are meaningful and appropriate for students. I will use a variety of activities to cater to my students' needs, including hands-on activities, learning centers, cooperative learning, and authentic learning tasks.

Standard 3: Diverse Learners Reflection

As an elementary teacher and a teacher of students with exceptionalities, I understand that creating learning experiences that encompass many different levels, modalities, and collaborative opportunities is in the best interest of my students. I will provide activities in the classroom that focus on the strengths of my students and will differentiate my instruction based on student strengths and needs.

Standard 4: Instructional Strategies Reflection

In every lesson that I design, I ensure that a variety of instructional strategies are used to best serve my students. Direct instruction, guided practice, cooperative learning, inquiry-based tasks, opportunities for independent practice, and open class discussion will be incorporated into all classroom activities.

Standard 5: Learning Environment Reflection

I want my students to claim ownership of their education, and that begins with claiming ownership of their learning environment. I will ensure that the classroom itself is designed and arranged to facilitate independent student learning. I will create learning centers that students can use independently during the school day. I will create an atmosphere of acceptance and security in my classroom, so that all students feel safe and supported in their learning endeavors.

Standard 6: Communication Reflection

I will use a variety of communication and media materials in my classroom to encourage my students to be involved with the world around them. These will include, but are not limited to, computers with Internet access, newspapers, magazines, videos, and other age-appropriate media.

Standard 7: Planning Instruction Reflection

Creating an educational environment that brings together the goals of the curriculum and the surrounding community lends itself to molding citizens who are actively involved in their community. As a teacher, I will create opportunities to actively involve my students in the community through community-based instruction and service learning, and I will also invite community members into the classroom to share in the education of my students.

Standard 8: Assessment Reflection

Assessment is the tool that drives effective instruction. Therefore, as a teacher, all instructional decisions I make in the classroom are based on assessment of previous topics taught and skills learned. I will use a variety of assessment tools in my classroom, such as observational checklists, probes, curriculum-based measures, and student feedback sessions.

Standard 9: Reflection and Professional Development Reflection

As a beginning teacher, I reflect following every lesson that I teach. I look at what worked in the lesson, improvements that can be made for future teachings of the lesson, procedural changes that may enhance the lesson, and any problems or concerns regarding student achievement of the lesson objectives. I also reflect on my overall teaching abilities, including classroom management, planning, lesson delivery, and cooperative efforts with other professionals in the field.

Standard 10: Collaboration, Ethics, and Relationships Reflection

An effective teacher understands that his or her role as an educator is twofold. Not only are we responsible for creating valuable learning experiences for and passing knowledge to our students but we also have a responsibility to the greater community. As teachers, it is our job to turn out students who are well rounded, involved, and invested in the world around them. To accomplish this goal, I will involve the community in my classroom through field trips, inviting community members into my classroom, and collaborating with community agencies to ensure that I am providing my students with the best practical experiences possible.

These reflections on the INTASC standards were the most challenging part of designing the e-portfolio for this preservice teacher. They say much about her philosophy of education and specifically outline what is important to her in the classroom. A viewer would have no difficulty deciding what this preservice teacher knows and intends to do. A benefit of this depth of reflection is that the artifacts selected to provide evidence of these understandings and beliefs naturally follow. The preservice teacher needs only to look at the collection of artifacts assembled and reflect on which ones demonstrate the standard and reflective belief on that standard.

The following are examples of questions that promote reflective thinking as teachers make decisions about portfolio contents:

- How do the artifacts in your portfolio represent your beliefs about teaching and learning?
- Do the artifacts demonstrate how effective you are in increasing student learning?
- Do the selected artifacts demonstrate your ability to differentiate instruction to meet the needs of diverse learners?

Such reflective questions help to determine whether educational standards are being met and how current practices can be improved. As teachers think critically about their practices and examine their actions and beliefs, it will become evident to them where their successes lie and where goals for continuing improvement need to be established.

Although there is no prescribed way to write a teaching portfolio, there must be strong evidence of honest reflection. It is quite acceptable to reflect on teaching activities that did not have the desired effect of improving student learning, as well as reflecting on those activities that were successful. The value of teacher self-assessment lies in teachers having a good, hard look at what they are doing; selecting artifacts that support their achievements; and presenting a plan for continuing development. Reflection and self-assessment come from within, and so does change.

❖ SELF-ASSESSMENT OPPORTUNITIES FOR STUDENTS

When students are first introduced to self-assessment, good teachers model the process of reflection and demonstrate the benefits of assessing one's own work. Initially, it will be difficult for students to make self-assessments on the quality of their own work because schools so rarely ask students to do so. As students begin to become self-directed in the act of self-assessment, they realize that the key to progress is in meeting the evaluation criteria for a product or process.

Self-assessment rubrics provide the questions and statements that focus students on their behaviors and accomplishments and should be incorporated into every portfolio. The students know the criteria for a task in advance. Figure 4.1 shows the criteria for following directions for a primary-level science journal.

The criteria for success should be clearly explained to students before and during their work. The teacher should read the criteria to

Figure 4.1   Student Self-Assessment for Plant Journal

Science Journal on Plants Student Self-Assessment		
Directions: Put a sticker above the words that best tell about your work.		
1. Did you write in your journal at least twice a week?	I did. Sometimes I did. Not at all.	
2. Did you illustrate each entry?	I did. Sometimes I did. Not at all.	
3. Did you share your observations with at least one other person?	I did. Sometimes I did. I did not.	
4. Did you use correct punctuation and capital letters in each entry?	I did. Sometimes I did. I need help.	

students as they complete the rubric by placing a sticker above the choice they feel best tells about their work. Self-assessment rubrics such as this one can be created for any task and can become the focal points for goal-setting conferences with the teacher. Once the self-assessment rubrics are included in the final portfolio, students can refer to them when presenting the portfolio to parents.

The student and the teacher can complete assessment rubrics, and the scores on the two rubrics can become the focus of a student-teacher conference. Figure 4.2 shows a rubric for a ninth-grade research project in a social studies class that was completed by the teacher.

The same rubric completed by the student may or may not have similar evidence. During the student-teacher conference, both the teacher and the student can discuss the reasons behind their scores. Giving students a chance to provide feedback on how and why they assessed their work as they did helps the teacher guide them toward realistic reflection. The student can then write a reflective commentary on the research process that addresses student strengths in the process and establishes goals for continuing improvement. This reflective commentary should be included in the portfolio. It is the student's choice whether to include the rubrics, as the rubrics were an avenue to deeper self-assessment and not an end in themselves. The reflective commentary can accompany the artifact created from the research strategies' task.

In secondary school, student-teacher conferences can be difficult to schedule due to the number of students each teacher has. An alternative to conferences with every student is the Best-Work Evaluation Form (see Figure 4.3).

The Best-Work Evaluation Form can accompany every artifact that students decide to include in their portfolios. Students could also use the forms to write a reflective commentary for use at the very beginning of the portfolio to show evidence of learning and growth as a result of completing unit work. Teachers can assist students in reflecting on their work by prompting them with self-assessment questions such as the following:

- Identify ways in which others helped you, such as classmates, teachers, or family members.
- If you were to begin this (assignment, project, task) again, what would you change or do differently?
- What specific advice would you give to next year's students before they begin this work?

Figure 4.2   Teacher-Completed Rubric for Research Strategies

---

Rubric for Research Strategies

1. The question the student writes and the way it is researched indicates thoughtfulness.

   (Highly demonstrated) Adequately demonstrated Poorly demonstrated

   Evidence: <u>The question narrows the subject enough for you to do it justice. You looked up related subjects with ease.</u>

2. The student works in a self-disciplined way.

   Highly demonstrated Adequately demonstrated (Poorly demonstrated)

   Evidence: <u>You came to me many times for reassurance that you were doing the right thing, although you seemed to know that your approach was correct. You seemed easily distracted by other students when working in the library.</u>

3. The student finds different sources of information.

   (Highly demonstrated) Adequately demonstrated Poorly demonstrated

   Evidence: <u>Three encyclopedia entries, one CD-ROM, two books, and an interview made the information in your notes comprehensive and interesting.</u>

4. The student organizes information and keeps a record of it as it is collected.

   (Highly demonstrated) Adequately demonstrated Poorly demonstrated

   Evidence: <u>The notebook you kept with printed copies and notes from readings was very complete.</u>

5. The end products reflect in-depth research.

   Highly demonstrated Adequately demonstrated (Poorly demonstrated)

   Evidence: <u>Although you had a variety of sources, the written paper reflected just one of those sources. Did you read everything you collected before writing?</u>

Figure 4.3   Best-Work Evaluation Form

Best-Work Evaluation Form

Student Name: _____

Title of Artifact: _____

Directions: Please write your answers to questions in complete, well-written sentences.

1. What about this artifact makes it your best work?

2. What new things did you learn from doing this task?

3. What would you change about the task or your final product if you were to do this task again?

4. What advice would you give to future students who were about to complete this task?

The teacher can review the forms and/or oral responses to gauge the reflective abilities of the student and, perhaps, to inform instruction on future lessons.

The importance of creating self-assessment opportunities for students cannot be overstated. Without self-assessment, the electronic portfolio simply becomes a technological repository for student work. Although the electronic portfolio is arguably an excellent storage system for student work, it is not a portfolio unless there is evidence of reflection and self-assessment on carefully selected artifacts. A bona fide student portfolio will assist students in developing critical thinking skills while learning to rely on their abilities to make assessment decisions.

Part II of this book will help new portfolio creators to use the above suggestions and guidelines effectively. It is important to remember to have an honest critique of your work by an impartial person before decisions are finalized and others view the completed electronic portfolio.

SUMMARY

Self-assessment and reflection are vital parts of learning and help portfolio developers to know what they know and are able to do. The use of self-assessment rubrics can assist students and teachers in the reflective process. Equally important, learners need to identify existing strengths and make goals for continuing improvement. An emotionally supportive environment is vital to success in self-assessment, and the focus of reflection should be on reflection and reasoning, not solely on "correctness" in learning.

The next chapter will address guidelines for design decisions and the issues surrounding presenting the portfolio to others. As one makes design decisions when creating the e-portfolio, design basics should be adhered to that typically involve color choices, font selection and size, and layout options.

QUESTIONS TO GUIDE E-PORTFOLIO PREPARATION

1. Discuss the importance to teachers of self-assessment through reflection.

2. How can a carefully designed rubric assist teachers and students in self-assessment?

3. Select one standard that will guide you in e-portfolio development. Write a reflective interpretation of what the standard means to you. Compare your reflection with that of your peers.

5

Presenting the Portfolio

Focus Questions

- Are there basic rules for a quality presentation?
- What resources are available to me as I make my design decisions?
- Who is the audience for student portfolios?
- How can a teacher portfolio be used in professional development?
- Will an e-portfolio help me during a job interview?

❖ INTRODUCTION

Presenting the e-portfolio as discussed in this chapter refers to a double meaning of *presentation:* (1) a visual representation of something as well as (2) the act of formally presenting something. Visual representation issues surrounding the design decisions made by the author of an e-portfolio will be addressed in this chapter in addition to things to consider when presenting the e-portfolio to the audience for whom it was written. An effective presentation does not happen automatically but rather is a product of careful research and decision making concerning presentation skills. Who among us has never sat through a visual presentation, regardless of the media used, that was mediocre simply because the visuals were either uninteresting or distracting?

Poorly designed visuals can definitely interfere with the intended communication. In today's world of technology, there must be few people indeed who have not witnessed a presentation such as this. Multimedia presentations can be compelling and persuasive, or they can be distracting and disappointing. Sometimes, the problem is organization of content; sometimes, it is the colors selected or the font type and size that command more attention than the content itself. Sometimes, it is the presenter who simply reads the text to the audience instead of elaborating, clarifying, or even paraphrasing the contents. Mediocre presentations can be avoided by attending to basic design concepts and making design decisions wittingly and deliberately.

❖ PRESENTATION SKILLS

After students and teachers have worked toward common standards, engaged in self-assessment activities, and selected artifacts, there are several things to consider when designing the electronic portfolio. The multimedia format of the electronic portfolio is rather new to most of those in teaching and learning; as such, examining the aspects of the multimedia format is necessary to producing effective presentations.

Electronic portfolios, as presented in this book, are intended to "stand alone" as a testament to performance skills, knowledge, and achievement. For this reason, the portfolio author should decide in advance on features such as the font, a color palette, graphics, and layout and adhere to these decisions throughout the process of creating the portfolio. The reader can refer to Chapter 2 for sample layout suggestions. The following suggestions represent common agreement about the basics of e-portfolio design.

Decisions About Font Size and Type

The text should be readable and readily comprehended. Williams (1994) suggests the use of sans serif fonts (Helvetica, Futura, and Ariel), or fonts with no small strokes, because they tend to appear heavier and bolder. These fonts should be simple and in large sizes, with titles being around 36 points and subtext around 24 points. A good test for font size is to print the presentation as a handout, six slides per page. If the slides on the handout are not easy to read, then they will not be easy to read on a 15-inch monitor. There should be no more than two or three types of fonts per presentation (Williams, 1994). Instead of using many fonts for emphasis, the use of boldface, italic, or underlining should be considered. However, all three of these should not be used for emphasis on the same piece of text. "More is better" is not a maxim that translates well to electronic portfolio design.

Decisions About Color

Color is primarily used to emphasize, differentiate, and add interest to a presentation. Most people, including those without an art background, do not realize that the relationships created by color are far more important than choosing a color one simply likes. Some colors work together, and others fight against each other, so establishing sound relationships between colors is the key to a good visual presentation (Halverson, 2000). For example:

• Warm colors (reds, oranges, yellows) tend to move toward the audience and should therefore be used for emphasis, whereas their complementary cool colors (blue greens and blues) can be used as background colors (Yost, 2000).

• The currently more agreeable pairings of visual complementary colors are lemon yellow versus blue violet, red orange versus cyan blue, and magenta versus green (although reds and greens are seen by people with color blindness as one color only). Therefore, a lemon yellow font, with the choice of lemon yellow serving to emphasize the message, would complement a blue violet background on a slide.

Graphics, Photos, and Video Clips

All visual entries should be as simple, clear, and clean as possible. They should be included in the portfolio only if they add interest and complement the purpose of the portfolio. It is important to remember that an overuse of graphics can easily distract from the purpose, even if they are pertinent to the purpose. As one is considering which graphics, photos, and video clips to include in the portfolio, a good rule of thumb is to ask someone to honestly critique the clarity and value of the collection. Photos and video clips tend to have deeper meaning to the person who has a vested interest in them and little meaning at all for an outsider. Although there will be a reflective piece and explanation linked to photos and video clips that will help in meaning making, an outside opinion on whether these artifacts lend value and clarity to the portfolio is always helpful.

It would behoove the portfolio author to maintain a consistent style with all of the above throughout the portfolio. Attending to these basic guidelines should enhance the electronic portfolio and increase a favorable response from the intended audience.

❖ ADDITIONAL RESOURCES FOR DESIGN DECISIONS

Fortunately, there are some excellent Internet Web sites and other resources to assist portfolio creators with presentation skills that will enhance the electronic portfolio. The following annotated list provides help with many presentation decisions that will augment the look and impact of the electronic portfolio:

- www.presentersonline.com/tutorial/powerpoint. This site is maintained by Epson Presenters Online, developed by Epson America Incorporated, and is devoted to comprehensive multimedia presentations for use with PowerPoint. There are numerous tutorials in all aspects of PowerPoint presentation skills such as graphics, fonts and text, sound and narration, and the use of tables and charts, to name a few.

- www.bitbetter.com/powerfaq.html. The A Bit Better Corporation is a small consulting firm helping companies communicate and create products with maximum impact. A Bit Better Corporation is also the creator and publisher of the Screen Beans clip art collections. The inclusion of this Web site does not necessarily promote the use of private companies to assist with design issues. Rather, this Web site presents answers to literally hundreds of questions concerning the use of PowerPoint. The questions are organized by the features contained in PowerPoint, so that locating your question is very easy. This is a very valuable reference site for both discovering how to do something and for troubleshooting purposes.

- www.webreference.com/new/color2.html. Jupitermedia Corporation is a provider of global real-time news, information, research, and media resources for information technology and Internet industry professionals. One does not have to be an "industry professional," however, to find this Web site very informative and user-friendly. Of particular interest is the page titled "Communicate With Color," which helps professionals and newbies alike to apply color principles for maximum audience response.

- www.colormatters.com. Color Professor J. L. Morton designed this Web site, which is all about the world of color. Topics range from exploring basic color theory to a wide range of the research on the effects of color. This information is invaluable for selecting colors for backgrounds and fonts to suit an audience as well as selecting colors that complement one another.

- www.webstyleguide.com. The *Web Style Guide,* by Patrick Lynch and Sarah Horton, is presented in full text at this site. The guide presents basic design principles for Web sites, many of which directly translate to work in PowerPoint. The chapters on typography, editorial style, and graphics have a great deal of useful information for electronic portfolio designers.

- Williams, R., & Tollet, J. (2000). *The non-designers Web book: An easy guide to creating, designing, and posting your own Web site* (2nd ed.). Berkeley, CA: Peachpit Press. This book, by Robin Williams and John Tollet, offers many explicit examples of the use of quality contrast, alignment, repetition, and proximity as design and layout decisions are being made. *Contrast* is defined as what pulls the viewer into a slide or page. Alignment techniques help to unify and organize the page, and repetition provides for continuity among the slides. Proximity is the relationship that items develop when they are close together. Throughout the discussion of these presentation concepts, the authors provide many quality and easy-to-understand examples of how concepts apply to text, graphics, font, layout, and color decisions.

❖ PRESENTING THE PORTFOLIO TO OTHERS

The electronic portfolio is completed. Now what? Although a portfolio that is not presented to others can still be a positive learning experience, actually presenting the portfolio can provide closure to an empowering process. Closure provides portfolio authors with a chance to organize perceptions so that they make sense, and preparing for a public presentation of one's work heightens this mental process. Artists complete portfolios of works with earnest focus to get ready for a juried show. News journalists present portfolios of their best work when applying for a plum assignment. Teachers can share portfolios with colleagues during a staff development day that focuses on the required purpose of the portfolio. Professors can meet with rank and tenure committees to present their portfolios and respond to questions from committee members. Students can celebrate the end of a unit of study by presenting their electronic portfolios to parents, friends, or members of another class. These are just a small number of possibilities for presenting the electronic portfolio to others. In this last chapter of Part I, possibilities for teacher presentation opportunities will be addressed, followed by the presentation options for students. Although this book will be used almost exclusively by teachers, it is important to keep in mind that once the process is successfully completed by a teacher, it easily becomes a process one can use with students at all levels.

❖ PRESENTATION OF TEACHER PORTFOLIOS

Technically, preservice teachers fall into the "student" category, but when they have completed student teaching, they are just a short time away from being credentialed. To move the reflective thinking of a student teacher into the realm of future decision making, student teachers should be asked to predict teaching and learning decisions for their first year of teaching. Imagining themselves as first-year teachers allows student teachers to discuss their own emerging styles of teaching rather than styles that they learned from their cooperating teachers. Therefore, preservice teachers, at the time of the exit portfolio, are regarded as beginning teachers. Because preservice teachers still have one foot in the world of students while the other foot is moving forward to employment opportunities, both the exit presentation and the interview presentation need to be considered.

Exit Portfolio Presentation

Exit portfolios are proficiency portfolios that are a collection of knowledge, performance, and reflection on learning to document one's professional growth during the completion of an education program. Exit portfolio presentations should occur soon after student teaching.

Review teams of two or three reviewers can be established that include student teacher supervisors, cooperating teachers, and education faculty members. The number of students will surely influence how this presentation is planned. Institutions that have a large number of student teachers may want to require that each student provide each member of his or her team with a CD-ROM or DVD that contains the electronic portfolio.

Each team member can then review the portfolio using the rubric in Figure 5.1, and one reviewer can collect and report the scores to the appropriate person in the schools, colleges, and departments of education. Schools with smaller numbers of student teachers might want to gather the review team together and review the portfolio at the same time. Written specific feedback from reviewers can accompany the rubric so that the student teacher has the opportunity to consider and use the feedback prior to using the portfolio as part of the interview process.

Interview Presentations

Before it is determined how an electronic portfolio is presented, it is necessary to look at typical hiring practices for new teachers so that information will not be duplicated. The hiring process still relies heavily on paper credentials and traditional forms of application. The following describes the usual locations of teacher candidate information:

Placement Office Credentials File	Résumé
	Letters of reference, professional and personal
	Transcript
Initial Application Package	Résumé
	Completed application form
	Copy of state certification
	Referees' addresses and contact information
	State certification test scores
	Employment history
	Official transcript

Figure 5.1 Scoring Rubric for an Electronic Teaching Portfolio

Criteria	Exemplary	Proficient	Partially Proficient	Incomplete	Points
Selection of artifacts that address teaching standards	9 points All artifacts are clearly and directly related to one or more of the teaching standards and provide evidence of professional practice.	6 points Most artifacts are related to one or more of the teaching standards and provide evidence of professional practice.	3 points Few artifacts are related to one or more of the teaching standards, and the evidence of professional practice is sometimes unclear.	0 points Most artifacts are unrelated to teaching standards.	
Reflections	9 points All reflections clearly describe why artifacts demonstrate achievement of each teacher standard and include professional growth goals for continued learning.	6 points Most of the reflections describe why artifacts demonstrate achievement of each teaching standard and include professional growth goals for future learning.	3 points A few reflections describe why artifacts demonstrate achievement of each teaching standard and include professional growth goals for future learning.	0 points No reflections describe why artifacts demonstrate achievement of each teaching standard, and professional growth goals for future learning are not included.	
Use of multimedia	9 points All of the photographs, graphics, sound, and/or video enhance reflective statements and are appropriate examples for one or more teaching standards. All audio and/or video files are edited with high-quality shots or sound and include proper voice projection, appropriate language, and clear delivery.	6 points Most of the photographs, graphics, sound, and/or video enhance reflective statements and are appropriate examples for one or more teaching standards. Most audio and/or video files are edited with high-quality shots or sound and include proper voice projection, appropriate language, and clear delivery.	3 points A few of the photographs, graphics, sound, and/or video enhance reflective statements and are appropriate examples for one or more teaching standards. A few of the audio and/or video files are edited with inconsistent clarity or sound and do not completely enhance the standard.	0 points The photographs, sounds, and/or videos do not enhance reflective statements and are inappropriate examples of one or more teaching standards or are distracting and detract from the content.	

Criteria	Exemplary	Proficient	Partially Proficient	Incomplete	Points
Captions	6 points Captions are clear with meanings communicated well and without apparent contradiction.	4 points Captions are clear to a viewer upon a careful read. Some captions are difficult to understand.	2 points Captions sometimes seem to be unclear as to the intent of the writer.	0 points Captions are not clear, are inaccurate, or do not communicate well in many instances.	
Ease of navigation	9 points User-friendly with all functions of buttons and hyperlinks made clear through labels and user instructions. All navigation aids work.	6 points Button and hyperlink functions all operate properly, but some navigation aids do not seem entirely clear, requiring careful reading.	3 points User needs to carefully follow somewhat obscure navigation directions, and some navigation seems difficult or does not operate properly.	0 points Users have a difficult time moving through the presentation due to unclear directions or multiple links that do not operate properly.	
Layout and text elements	6 points Presentation is pleasing to the eye, using colors, text, and graphics in mutually reinforcing and uncluttered arrangements.	4 points Presentation uses a color-complementary color scheme, yet some slides seem to be cluttered with unnecessary text or graphics.	2 points Presentation does not use complementary colors, yet all is readable. Some slides have elements that clutter the portfolio.	0 points Presentation uses color that is not complementary or is difficult to see. Some elements seem out of place in the layout.	
Writing mechanics	9 points The writing is standard English, using accepted rules of spelling, grammar, construction, and syntax.	6 points The writing is standard English, but some errors in spelling, grammar, construction, and syntax detract from the presentation.	3 points The writing is standard English, yet frequent errors in spelling, grammar, construction, and syntax present a serious detractor.	0 points The writing does not use standard English, with frequent errors in spelling, grammar, construction, and syntax.	

These documents fill the role as a first-level screening tool. Semifinalists are selected as a result of using a screening technique such as looking at critical documents absolutely necessary for obtaining employment as a teacher. Semifinalists are then invited to an interview, usually with the school principal. A single candidate may be selected as a result of this interview, or the pool may be narrowed to two or three finalists. A final interview is scheduled that sometimes asks the prospective teachers to plan and teach a short lesson, but this practice of looking at performance is not yet common. Researchers Kardos and Liu (2003) surveyed a random sample of 486 new teachers in California, Florida, Massachusetts, and Michigan to learn about the hiring practices these teachers experienced. According to the study, only 7.5% of these teachers taught a sample lesson as part of the hiring process. In addition, findings from the Harvard Graduate School of Education's Project on the Next Generation of Teachers (Birkeland et al., 2001) indicated that 33% of new teachers are hired after the school year has started, and 62% are hired within 30 days of when they start teaching. Clearly, immediate attention needs to be paid to hiring practices that are conducted in a last-minute fashion. Such practices rely on the assessments of others or can result in a school being misled by a candidate who gives an appealing social impression during interviews such as these.

One strong advantage of the portfolio is that it can be viewed at the convenience of the interviewers. The time restrictions for performance-based interviews created by last-minute hiring practices can be lessened by requiring an electronic portfolio from semifinalists or finalists. Teachers, administrators, and parents on an interviewing team could view the portfolios as preparation for final interviews, thus providing all participants with a richer discussion forum. Many prospective teachers have asked us about the extent to which employers use electronic portfolios. At present, this is difficult to answer because there has been little empirical research on how teachers are being hired or on teachers' experiences during the hiring process. In a 2002 survey conducted by researchers at the University of Iowa, employers were asked to share their perceptions of e-portfolio content relative to prospective candidates' preparation, experience, and potential for success (Anthony & Roe, 2002). More than 200 practicing administrators from school districts in urban, suburban, small city, and rural settings responded to the survey questions. Almost all administrators gave the highest rankings to desiring e-portfolios that demonstrate an understanding of how students learn, provide confirmation of effective communication with

students, and show a command of a variety of instructional strategies by the prospective teacher. Clearly, employers expect to find
authentic documentation of student experience, training, and professional consciousness. More than 81% of the respondents indicated that
an e-portfolio is an important selection tool in the hiring process.
Researchers found that the majority of employers prefer to review
the e-portfolio before the interview, but they also caution that
e-portfolio quality can increase *or* diminish a candidate's employment chances. Thus, the importance of thoughtful design decisions
as well as content selection is reflective of how employers see you as
a prospective employee.

Although requesting electronic e-portfolios is on the rise, it is still
not as prevalent as it should be. It appears that the last-minute hiring
practices of many school districts need to be addressed if hiring teams
are going to assess the performance of new teachers, which is essential
to hiring quality teachers. Because most districts rely on paper credentials for the initial application, the letter of application should promote
your electronic portfolio by identifying key examples of your work that
you would like employers to view. The decision to send the electronic
portfolio with the initial application depends on the individual district's application procedures. Some districts clearly state that they do
not want any extra materials beyond those stated in the application
package. A good rule of thumb is to include the CD-ROM electronic
portfolio when this is not the case. The portfolio label should have all
identifying information clearly presented as well as a note about operating instructions (i.e., "may be used in any computer"). Even if no one
views the electronic portfolio at this time, the message is sent that the
teacher candidate for hire has technology and organizational skills. If
the teacher candidate passes the screening interview, then copies of the
electronic portfolio can be given to each member of the interviewing
team. If school districts request a portfolio, then the teacher candidate
should follow the application guidelines.

❖ PRESENTATION OF STUDENT PORTFOLIOS

For students in elementary school, it is a good idea to plan the culmina-
tion of the portfolio to coincide with report card time and required conferences with parents. This will give teachers a chance to demonstrate
their student-centered approach to parents as well as inform the parents

about student performance that has led to a grade on the report card. The outcome of such a practice serves to increase the collaborative behaviors between the teacher and the families of their students. The student, as the author of the electronic portfolio, is at the center of this approach. Given that students are at the center of the learning process and that parent involvement is highly desirable, the following illustrates possible steps that could be taken in a classroom that uses portfolio assessment and that has student empowerment as a major goal (Montgomery, 2001):

- In advance of teaching an integrated unit of study from which the electronic portfolio is derived, the teacher sends a letter to parents that describes the tasks that students will complete. The letter also invites parents to contribute to learning in any way they can.
- The teacher appropriately incorporates suggestions and assistance from parents into the unit plan.
- Students proceed through the unit work and create a best-work electronic portfolio after reflection on their achievements that includes goals for continuing improvement. The goal-setting form (see Figure 5.2) can provide an organizing structure for students that can be presented to parents.
- The students and teacher plan a "Portfolio Party" upon completion of the electronic portfolio and invite parents or others to be the audience for their portfolio presentation.
- The party can take place in the classroom and the computer room. If there is no computer room, the teacher can gather as many computers as possible, and participants can take turns showing the electronic portfolio and eating and socializing.
- A goal of this presentation is for parents to become aware of existing strengths in their children's learning and assist their children with implementing their goals for continuing improvement.
- At the student/parent/teacher report card conference, all classroom work throughout the reporting period will be addressed, but the focus will now be on the student's goal-setting results. Parents and the teacher can make sure that the goals are realistic, add more goals, and discuss ways in which they can assist the student in meeting these goals.

These guidelines for electronic portfolio presentations can be modified in any way the teacher wishes. For example, if a teacher determines that the chance of getting almost all parents to come to school for the presentation party is not very good, then other avenues

Figure 5.2   Goal-Setting Form for Use With Elementary Students

---

Goal-Setting Form

Student Name: _____

Date: _____

1. I have shown the following strengths in my work.

2. I have the following goals for improvement in my work.

3. This is what I will do to help me meet my goals.

4. This is how my teacher and parents can help me to meet my goals.

In a few weeks, I will meet with my parents at home and we will talk about how well I am meeting my goals. I will report what we talked about to my teacher.

_____

Student signature

NOTE: Students can discuss the questions on this form with the teacher and parents and complete all items. All parties can add comments and suggestions at a student-parent-teacher conference.

for audiences need to be explored. Students could invite another class or a group of adults from the school (i.e., principal, school nurse, counselor, lunch aide, other teachers, or janitors). Regardless of who the audience is, students get a chance to share and talk about their finished work, which is a very important component of goal setting.

Portfolio presentations for secondary students need to be structured differently because of the large number of students a teacher has in addition to the rather nonnegotiable daily schedule normally found in middle and high schools. Teachers who collaborate on units and the electronic portfolios that come from unit work can arrange for an exchange of portfolio presentations between their classes. Some high schools require that all seniors complete a senior project. This requirement would seem to lend itself nicely to an e-portfolio presentation format.

❖ PROFESSIONAL DEVELOPMENT PRESENTATIONS

Imagine any K–12 school where teachers, administrators, and support personnel decided to complete electronic portfolios over a year's time in lieu of the regular, and sometimes hodgepodge, staff development in-services that normally occur. The in-service calendar and funds would all be devoted to teacher-created electronic portfolio development. The purpose of the portfolio could be to examine one's own teaching style, to look at how a specific district requirement was being fulfilled, or simply to give teachers the authentic task of demonstrating the portfolio process. The latter would be particularly useful if teachers are expected and encouraged to use portfolio assessment with their students.

Throughout the year, teachers can learn the skills necessary to complete an electronic portfolio, and they can meet with colleagues to discuss their progress and engage in peer review of their work in progress. At the end of the year, teachers can present their portfolios within grade-level teams, to content department teams, or to the entire faculty. It should be noted that this should not be viewed as a formal part of the teacher evaluation process but as an opportunity for teachers to learn from one another. This exercise can do much toward promoting a climate of reflection, self-assessment, goal setting, and sharing that is at the heart of the electronic portfolio process. As a character in *Alice in Wonderland* said, "If you don't know where you're going, any road will take you there." In education, we need to know exactly where we are going, and standards-based electronic portfolios will take us there.

SUMMARY

E-portfolios should be presented to an audience to provide evidence of what the portfolio creator knows and is able to do. The audience can be peers, parents, colleagues, interviewing teams, or rank and tenure committees. The purpose for creating the e-portfolio should be clear and apparent to the audience. This chapter offered many kinds of e-portfolio presentation opportunities as well as things to consider when preparing for a presentation.

An electronic portfolio (e-portfolio) can be prepared in many formats, but the focus of Part II will be on the widely available and widely used PowerPoint program by Microsoft. Part II will assist teachers and students in selecting the media that will best showcase the artifacts. This section will briefly review a number of programs that can be used for portfolio preparation but will focus on PowerPoint by Microsoft as a commonly used and widely available platform for the construction of a portfolio. Chapters will include PowerPoint basics, planning an e-portfolio, selecting formats for files that will be used as artifacts in the portfolio, producing and editing graphics, preparing the portfolio using the PowerPoint program, and burning the portfolio to CD or DVD media.

QUESTIONS TO GUIDE E-PORTFOLIO PREPARATION

1. Clearly describe the audience for your e-portfolio. List the expectations this audience will have for a good e-portfolio.

2. With your audience in mind, determine two or three colors that will complement your e-portfolio and determine the font you will use.

3. With your peers, determine the possible ways in which you can present your portfolio to the intended audience.

PART II

Using PowerPoint to Author E-Portfolios

6

Options for
Electronic Portfolios

Focus Questions

- What are the options for preparing an e-portfolio?
- What are the advantages and disadvantages of using Web-based portfolio tools?
- Why is PowerPoint the program of choice in this book?

❖ INTRODUCTION

A variety of choices confront a learner once the decision is made to use an e-portfolio. The question, however, should focus on one primary assumption. One must remember that the objective of any portfolio is to document learning, but if that documentation is contained in an e-portfolio, a major concern is that the e-portfolio can be viewed. A university program that uses a commercial Web-based tool for a program exit e-portfolio will not necessarily work well for practicing teachers in the preparation of an e-portfolio for use in documenting their professional development efforts. Similarly, the use of a very sophisticated authoring tool may not be best for use by a teacher with children in class. In addition, the use of any tool that is difficult to import into other applications or settings may not be the best choice in the development of an e-portfolio for interview purposes. Therefore, the assumption in making a decision regarding which of the available e-portfolio authoring tools is best for your use must be focused on the need for the tool to be easily accessible by the writer and by the writer's intended audience. With this assumption, a review of some of the options should be undertaken.

Many of the e-portfolio programs that are on the market are based on commercially prepared Web-based products or user-authored Web pages. Other products used to produce e-portfolios are based on tools that are "local" or individual computer applications normally used as presentation software programs rather than based on Web technology. Many of these "local" tools are presentation programs commonly found among the contents of most "all programs" listings familiar to computer users but are adaptable for the production of e-portfolios. These include PowerPoint (favored by the authors), WordPerfect's Presentations, or Open Office Impress. Furthermore, "local" tools can be of equal or superior value to commercial Web-based products. Local production of e-portfolios offers the author an opportunity to work in an environment in which many already have some familiarity, yet it also has the capability to present each of the standards separately, offer related reflections, and even hyperlink to student-selected and appropriate artifacts external to the e-portfolio presentation. The use of hyperlinking internally to the presentation can result in a presentation not unlike a Web page with navigation among a table of contents, standards, reflections, and artifacts, but with the security that is inherent in locally maintained files. The decision as to which of the e-portfolio options to use is summarized in Table 6.1.

This chapter will review some of the more common programs for the generation of e-portfolios, discuss the platforms used, and provide details as to characteristics of alternative authoring tools. All of this is provided to clarify the factors considered that have led to the choice of PowerPoint as the authoring tool that will be used throughout the remainder of this book.

❖ WEB-BASED E-PORTFOLIO TOOLS

Web-based e-portfolios are quite common. They have been written for and mounted to a server for viewing via the Internet, and they have the

Table 6.1   E-Portfolio Authoring Tools

Options	Advantages	Disadvantages
Web pages authored by the author	Author choice is maximized Creativity is maximized	Each author has different product Security issues Server space and file maintenance
Web templates that authors utilize	Authors have some choice Author products appear standard	Security issues Server space and file maintenance
Commercial Web-based templates	Authors choose required artifacts Server space and file maintenance off-site	Additional fee for authors Security issues
Local multimedia tools	Author choice is maximized Creativity is maximized No required server or file maintenance Can be mounted to the Web	Requires choice of application program Viewer must have application or import into a common application

clear advantage of being easily accessible by anyone with a Web browser such as Netscape Navigator or Microsoft Internet Explorer. The presentation of this type of e-portfolio involves starting the browser, navigating to the appropriate URL, and viewing the e-portfolio as any other Web presentation. These portfolios all have a structure that is nonlinear, just as the Web is nonlinear. The use of hyperlinks and buttons can enable a viewer to go to content of particular interest without having to navigate through other content that is not of the same degree of interest. In this way, a viewer does not necessarily need to progress through the portfolio as if it were a more structured presentation. A viewer can opt to jump around the portfolio from one section to another based on the viewer's need or preference. This structure is graphically represented in Figure 6.1.

One version of the Web-based e-portfolio is the self-designed and self-authored page. This type of portfolio uses an approach that is the equivalent of creating a sequence of Internet pages. In days not so long ago, a Web page author needed to first learn hypertext markup language (HTML), the language shared by virtually all computer platforms for the composition, reading, and display of Web pages. HTML was not difficult to learn: The user simply needed to add specific "tags" to lines and sections, which served to control the display position, size, and color contained in the page. Now, the construction of a Web-based e-portfolio is even more painless with the advent of page-authoring tools such as Netscape Composer or Microsoft Front Page. Users need not be concerned with adding "tags" as these page-authoring tools will do that for the user.

Using commonly recognized navigation tools, an e-portfolio author could create a version of the Web-based portfolio in the same way that any Web site is created. The Curry School (of the University of Virginia) Center for Technology and Teacher Education and Penn State University are sources of several examples of Web-based portfolios. Using the following URLs, a viewer can get a good idea of the promise and limitations of this type of portfolio:

http://curry.edschool.virginia.edu/class/edlf/589-07/sample.html

http://portfolio.psu.edu/about/index.html

The University of Wisconsin at La Crosse (UW-L) uses a Web-based system in which the candidate is provided a template of required contents and format and allows each candidate to make choices regarding his or her reflections and artifacts. This example establishes a standard presentation of the candidate's work, which, in turn, has the strength of allowing for more familiarity on the part of each evaluator. Using the following URLs, a viewer can follow the links to the templates for the UW-L or Kennesaw State University e-portfolio system:

http://www.uwlax.edu/soe/portfolio/information.htm

http://www.kennesaw.edu/university_studies/sye/pocket.shtml

Each candidate who has posted a Web-based e-portfolio has, in effect, designed a Web site that presents his or her own information—information that the candidate chooses, formats, and mounts to the Web site. The ability to move from section to section in a nonlinear manner is a strength of these e-portfolios. Given the relative ease of constructing Web pages with the Web design tools mentioned earlier, and given that most people know how to navigate the Web, the Web-based portfolio has the obvious value of familiarity.

Figure 6.1   A Diagram of the Nonlinear Pathways Available in Web-Based E-Portfolios

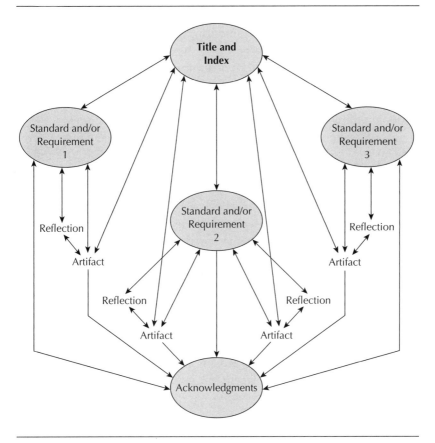

NOTE: A Web-based e-portfolio allows navigation in a nonlinear manner that permits the reader to jump from feature to feature in a wide variety of pathways among three standards and four artifacts.

Figure 6.1 graphically represents the navigation within this type of Web-based portfolio. Many pages are published when one authors this type of e-portfolio. Some may contain a title with an index, standards, or requirements that are set for the e-portfolio; artifacts that are selected to demonstrate that the standards are met; and an acknowledgments page to recognize contributors or materials that require permission. Links are established from the index to the various standards, then to reflections, where the e-portfolio author explains how they demonstrate that the standards were met and which artifacts are selected to verify the reflection. Links are added to lead the reviewer from the reflections to the individual artifacts. The reflections are important in that they are the crux of the matter, including information more important than the artifacts themselves. Knowing why a candidate selects a specific artifact is important as a more authentic means of assessing a candidate's reflection as to how he or she meets the standard. In an e-portfolio, links can be established to allow the viewer to move directly between the index and each standard and artifact. A diagram of this kind of e-portfolio would appear as a web because the optional pathways that a viewer might choose are numerous.

Another version of the Web-based e-portfolio uses either a commercial provider or noncommercial program to establish a template that can be used to add a common structure to the portfolio. The structure of the template may be based on locally developed standards or requirements, or the structure may be based on state or national standards. The primary difference in this version of the Web-based e-portfolio is the structure. In the first version discussed, each Web-based e-portfolio had a unique appearance and its own structure for the Web page as it displayed on the computer screen. In the second version, a structure was established, but the choice of content and artifact was still left to the candidate. In this third version of the Web-based e-portfolio, each of the portfolios has the same appearance as it is viewed and the nature of each artifact is specified. The following addresses will take the reader to the Web sites of TaskStream and Chalk and Wire electronic portfolio systems. These represent one commercial option for the construction of a Web-based e-portfolio system.

https://www.taskstream.com/pub/

http://www.chalkandwire.com/eportfolio/

In most cases, the portfolio author has access to a secured Web site that contains the e-portfolio template. The security precautions vary widely but are usually password protected to limit access to each user's own file. Each author pays a subscription that allows him or her to post the content selected as appropriate into the template and then save the e-portfolio into a separate space. This space is most often a defined allotment of memory at a remote site. The allotment is protected from viewing from others (partitioned), with access limited to only specific persons. The partitioned memory usually exists in the memory of a network or Web-accessed server dedicated to the purpose of saving portfolio authors' work. Each partitioned space is normally

only accessible to the author, the supervisor of the portfolio requirement (course instructor, administrator, or assessment coordinator), and
the computing system supervisor. Although each system has its own
specific bells and whistles, this is the most common design of the template version of the Web-based e-portfolio. The subscription required
for each candidate explains how the service is a dot-com.

Using any version of the Web-based e-portfolio (author designed
or template), the e-portfolio can be viewed using any of the widely
available Web navigation tools. In some cases, the e-portfolio is posted
and can then be reviewed by anyone who has access to the page
through the Internet. This is a strength of the Web-based e-portfolio, for
any Web-capable machine has access from any point in the world
where access is possible, with only Web-browsing software being necessary once the machine is connected to the Web. In addition, the use
of dedicated servers and partitioned space has the potential to generate information in specific report formats. All of the answers posted to
a specific requirement or standard could be separated from all else and
reported without being linked to specific authors. This capability has
tremendous value when those who set the requirements or those who
establish the standards choose to examine the range and nature of data
posted to answer any specific requirement or standard.

The devil in all of this, however, is in the detail. In this case, security is always a concern in that, as the name implies, posting the page
to the Web exposes the page to a potential worldwide audience. This
strength also presents an obvious danger as an author's e-portfolio may
contain information far too sensitive for such a wide audience. Not
limited to personal information that may be contained in an author's
résumé, the danger of exposure extends to additional details. The artifacts may include images, writings, or creative products of the author
or others. Although permission to use such artifacts in an e-portfolio
should be secured as a responsibility of the author, the dissemination of
such items to a potential worldwide audience may not be desirable.

Although Internet security is better now than ever before, there are
still those in our society who revel in their ability to break into secured
sites. They may do so for the entertainment, enjoyment, or covert purposes of altering information, stealing identification, or implanting
viruses that can be shared through the hardware enabling the
Web-based tools being used. In many of the examples of Web-based
e-portfolios on sites presently on the Web, résumés were found to contain
far too much personal information. Although the Web-based e-portfolio
has obvious strengths, especially as related to assessment and maintenance

arenas, the risks may outweigh the benefits of posting materials to the Web. It is recommended that e-portfolios authored in this way be saved locally on appropriate computer media without being posted. The media could be computer floppy disks, CDs, DVDs, or a local-area network server not accessible through the Web. Materials saved in this way can still be viewed with the navigation tools mentioned previously. For the purposes of this discussion, an important question remains as to whether it is possible to develop Web-based e-portfolios that do not have the risk that the World Wide Web may present.

❖ NON–WEB-BASED (LOCAL) E-PORTFOLIO TOOLS

Non–Web-based e-portfolios are based on computer programs that are usually intended to be presentation tools. These tools include the popular HyperStudio, Apple's Keynote, and the widely used PowerPoint, commonly a part of the Microsoft Office package. Presentation software clarifies a presentation, with projected information containing notes or lists that serve to augment the presentation. It would be difficult to find someone who has not observed a demonstration of presentation software, which is commonly used to augment an otherwise normal presentation. In the worst use of the technology, the software is used to supply the presenter with text that he or she then reads to the audience. A more suitable use of this technology is to enhance a presentation by presenting an outline, stressing important points, or supplying information that adds to a good presentation. Thus, the presentation software creates, in a sense, a more modern, high-tech, more attractive, and more easily altered overhead transparency.

Presentation programs are increasingly popular and are now a common feature in our schools. Even elementary school children are taught how to use the program for their assignments. PowerPoint (the well-known product of Microsoft), Keynote (an Apple Corporation version of a PowerPoint-like presentation software package), HyperStudio (a multimedia authoring tool more capable but less common than PowerPoint), and other such presentation tools have a number of commonly used options. They might allow, for example, stepwise revealing of information, with the selected information not appearing instantly but only after a cue provided by timing or a mouse click. Other common tools include graphics and music options along with options to create special effects as slides change. These programs may also permit the addition of the author's voice to the presentation. These programs are common and fairly easy to use. Access is dependent on simply owning a copy of the software and having suitable hardware to run the program. The widespread use of these programs is demonstrated in that many computers come packaged with presentation software. For those who need to see the presentation but do not have the software, many programs have a free "reader" that can be downloaded for viewing.

In that most presentation software is treated as a linear program, the most common use of the programs is to move from one slide to the next, in a specific order. Although there are other options available within these programs, it is uncommon in practice to use the program for anything other than a linear presentation. A diagram showing a linear presentation format is presented in Figure 6.2. In this diagram, the title page is located on the top left, and as the presentation unfolds, the slides are revealed, in order, from the title page across to the right, then down and across to the left. The diagram as developed shows the same three standards and four artifacts that were used in Figure 6.1. The difficulty in using presentation software in a traditional format is that the viewer of the portfolio needs to do one of two things to see the fourth artifact. The viewer must either choose to go through nearly the entire presentation, or the viewer needs to stop, find the built-in navigation tool, and then move to the desired slide if the slide title is known. The advantage of presentation software is that it is relatively easy to use, and it does not need to be viewed using a Web site or Web navigation tool. Security is less of an issue using this software.

Advanced features of presentation software are far less common in most uses of the packages. Such features include attaching the author's own music or graphics, which may include still pictures as well as movie clips. The author can also include a feature that allows the viewer to "jump" from slide to slide, or slide to a document outside of the presentation software, and then jump back to the original or to a different slide. This feature, known as hyperlinking, can be used to move both within the program and to documents outside of the presentation. The author can create hyperlinks either by allowing the viewer to click on the words describing where the hyperlink will go (in a manner similar to most Web page navigation) or by creating a series of "buttons" that can be "pushed" by clicking on the button. Hyperlinks can be established to view documents or to move from the presentation software to specific Web addresses. Within the parameters of e-portfolios, most hyperlinking is used to navigate through the e-portfolio and to link to documents, graphics, or sound that might comprise the artifacts selected for inclusion.

Figure 6.2   A Diagram of the Linear Pathway of a Typical PowerPoint
Presentation

Start

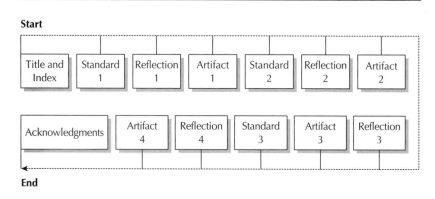

End

NOTE: A linear presentation model requires information to be presented in a set sequence or order. This is the typical model involved in the use of presentation software, here representing three standards and four artifacts.

The use of hyperlinking can alter the more traditional use of presentation software by making it appear less linear. The ability of a viewer to move to a specific page in the presentation is the equivalent of a Web-based portfolio viewer selecting the page containing the standard of interest. A viewer may not be interested in the record of achievement composed under one standard but may be interested in the performance assessment, which could be located on a later page. The ability to jump around information and to move directly to that performance assessment from an index allows the viewer to save time—often the most valuable commodity. Figure 6.3 includes the use of this feature within presentation software, allowing the viewer to jump between and among hyperlinked pages of the presentation in a nonlinear manner.

Figure 6.3 shows how to use the traditional features of presentation software to establish the same three standards used in earlier diagrams, Figures 6.1 and 6.2. However, to read reflections and see the artifacts, the viewer can click on a hyperlink and be transported to any point in the presentation from the index or to related reflections and/or artifacts included in the e-portfolio. The viewer has the option, of course, to click and simply move through the presentation, but that would imply that many aspects of the e-portfolio residing outside of the presentation might be missed. Thus, in authoring a portfolio using the advanced features of the presentation software, the portfolio author must take into account that a viewer may not automatically know

Figure 6.3   Diagram Showing a PowerPoint Presentation as a Linear
Pathway (Dashed Line) Made More Nonlinear (Solid Line)
With Hyperlinks

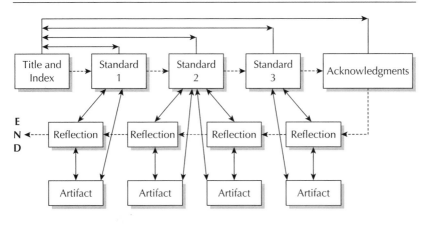

NOTE: This nonlinear presentation format will run as a normal presentation along the dashed line but can use hyperlinks to become less linear along solid lines. This model presents three standards with four artifacts.

to move through the presentation to reflections and artifacts. The portfolio author needs to supply sufficient information in the design of the portfolio to allow for this movement.

Table 6.2 contains a list of selected portfolio authoring systems. Reflected in the table are several factors that influence their use in any portfolio effort. The list is broken into two broad categories and is not, by any means, represented as a complete listing of tools available. In fact, under the heading of "Web-Based" tools, three programs are reviewed. These three are only a portion of a very large number of tools now being used or developed. A recent Web search found that there are, literally, thousands of e-portfolio development tools on the market. In fact, many of the commercial vendors of e-portfolio tools are engaged in customizing their sites to a point that their product is available in a number of formats. What is needed at one company or institution is not necessarily what is desirable at another company or institution due to differences in missions or systems of standards. Furthermore, many of these e-portfolio tools are available in non–Web-based versions. Although the list should be able to demonstrate the range of options available to the e-portfolio author, it is important to recognize that the half-dozen included e-portfolio tools represent a very limited selection.

Table 6.2   Choices of Selected Common E-Portfolio Authoring Tools in Terms of Some User and Authoring Tool Characteristics

	User Requirements			
	Level of Computer Literacy Required	*Creativity Required*	*Cost of Use*	*Benefits/Limitations*
Web based				
Netscape	High	High	Free	Low cost—difficult to use
Task Stream	High	Moderate	Subscription	Turnkey—limits creativity
Macromedia Cold Fusion	High	High	High	Somewhat difficult to use
Non-Web based				
KidPixs	Low	High	Cost of program	Easy use limits features
HyperStudio	High	Moderate	Cost of program	Somewhat difficult to use
Macromedia Director	High	High	Cost of program	Somewhat difficult to use
Apple Keynote	Moderate	High	Cost of program	Macintosh platform only
Easy Presentations	Moderate	High	Cost of program	Not used as widely as PowerPoint
Open Office Impress	Moderate	High	Free download	Easy conversion to other formats
WordPerfect Presentations	Moderate	High	Cost of program	Often preinstalled on new computers
MS PowerPoint	Moderate	High	Cost of program	Widely used program

❖ SELECTING A PORTFOLIO TOOL

The portfolio author needs to consider several variables in selecting a portfolio tool that is to be used for a specific reason. These variables provide a picture of the needs established by the portfolio requirement and together produce a profile unique to each setting. The portfolio author should consider factors ranging from the technological preparation of the anticipated viewer and the author to the intended use of the portfolio. It is evident from the list contained in Table 6.1 that the characteristics of the selected e-portfolio tools describe an obvious trade-off between ease of use and the supported features. If a program is relatively easy to use, the options that an author has are limited by the features that are supported by the technology. KidPixs, for example, is a relatively easy-to-use program that allows young children to compose rudimentary multimedia presentations. KidPixs is a logical choice for elementary schools that have students with limited technological literacy or for schools with limited technology that would make posting the e-portfolio to the Web less likely. This choice would address the limitations of the users while limiting the choices and complexities that may make other programs too difficult.

Alternatively, if a software developer wishes to develop an e-portfolio to demonstrate all of the complex options that can be present in an e-portfolio system, and if that developer wishes to post the e-portfolio to the Web, a more sophisticated program may be the better choice. For example, if the developer is a more advanced user, the options in a "Cold Fusion" application would allow more options for a more spectacular site. Cold Fusion is a presentation authoring tool that offers more options than most e-portfolio authors might need. This is not to say that an easier program is incapable of producing a spectacular e-portfolio—it is simply that not all e-portfolio authors will need the variety of "bells and whistles" available in the advanced e-portfolio tools.

The following specific questions should be asked when deciding which tool should be used to develop e-portfolios:

1. *What are the requirements or standards to be used as a basis of the e-portfolio?* The e-portfolio will be based on a set of requirements or standards. If these are extensive, requiring a more complex presentation, then the e-portfolio will need to be less "easy" and more sophisticated for the e-portfolio's development.

2. *What are the expected artifacts that will be needed to support the e-portfolio?* Before selecting the e-portfolio tool to be used, e-portfolio authors should consider the kinds of artifacts that may be selected. This examination will feed into the next question.

3. *What are the expected formats of artifacts that will need to be supported?* If the artifacts are to include a variety of graphics, music, and navigation options, then there will be an equivalent need to choose a tool that will support an equally wide variety of formats.

4. *What is the technological ability of the author of the e-portfolios?* To submit high-quality portfolios, the portfolio author must be prepared to use the tool selected, the platform on which it is running (Windows vs. Macintosh), and the technology that will support the production of the digital files that will serve as artifacts in the e-portfolio.

5. *What is the level of technology available in the infrastructure?* A failed effort is sure to follow the selection of a tool that is beyond the capability of the infrastructure available to the e-portfolio author. If authors are to use a Web-based system, and the system is not available to off-site work due to infrastructure limitations, the e-portfolio may not be as complete as it would with such access.

❖ POWERPOINT AS AN E-PORTFOLIO DEVELOPMENT TOOL

The immediate question that needs to be addressed is, What does this book recommend as an e-portfolio development tool? Remembering the primary assumption established earlier, and following the five-question schema listed above, the result is a set of parameters for the remainder of the book. The process of decision making in this instance is presented in Table 6.3. In this case, technology is not a limiting factor, except that long-term Web page storage could present a difficulty. The technological preparation of Web authors is not an insurmountable challenge in terms of selecting an e-portfolio authoring tool. Implicit in this is whether e-portfolio authors could be prepared to use the selected tool within a time frame that is both realistic and reasonable. Also implicit is that e-portfolio authors will not be prepared to use very sophisticated authoring tools. Because there is a potentially large variety of formats in which artifacts may need to be included in the e-portfolio, there needs to be a fairly high number of features supported by the e-portfolio tool selected. The combination of considerations in this case leads one to conclude that an authoring tool that is neither the most nor the least sophisticated would be required. For that reason, the remainder of the book will focus on presentation software prepared by Microsoft. PowerPoint is both widely available and will support a large number of artifact formats.

Table 6.3   A Consideration of Needs for Choosing an E-Portfolio Authoring Tool

Question	Consideration
1. What are the requirements or standards to be used as a basis of the portfolio?	The standards will be fairly extensive as they will be geared to a teacher preparation program or exit criteria, yet customized to allow for the adoption of a variety of educational or business applications.
2. What are the expected artifacts that will be needed to support the portfolio?	Artifacts are sure to contain still pictures, video clips, music, and a variety of word-processed documents as well as scanned forms.
3. What are the expected formats of artifacts that will need to be supported?	Documents will most likely be in MS Word and Excel, JPG scanned formats, digitally captured video, music, and/or voice files.
4. What is the technological ability of the authors of the portfolios?	Most users of the technology will be familiar with the basics of computer applications but less familiar with Web-based tools and posting of Web pages that are self-designed.
5. What is the level of technology available in the infrastructure?	Infrastructure is not a limiting factor as sufficient equipment is in place at most teacher preparation sites to support the short-range "local" development activities of e-portfolios. However, the long-term storage of pages online could represent a limitation.

Using PowerPoint as the tool for e-portfolio authoring has several advantages. PowerPoint presentations can be mounted to and accessed by the Web but are more commonly saved to media. In this book, we will introduce a variety of media that can be used to save PowerPoint presentations, including flash drives, hard disk drives, and servers. We will also consider the means by which presentations can be saved as optical media (in a process known as "burning" due to the use of lasers) such as CD-ROM or DVD presentations. The remainder of the book, then, will be a step-by-step "how-to" guide for basic portfolio presentations using PowerPoint as the preparation tool.

SUMMARY

The production of e-portfolios has an advantage over other kinds of physical portfolios in that the e-portfolio can be easily duplicated and is easily stored. There are two major types of e-portfolios—Web based and non-Web based. Web-based portfolios use Web authoring tools and are saved to servers, making them widely accessible. Non–Web-based portfolios use presentation software and more fully use the creative capabilities of the portfolio authors. Since a security concern may exist with Web-based e-portfolios, more control can be ensured with non–Web-based options. Microsoft's PowerPoint—one of the more common presentation software packages, available across platforms—will be used for the remainder of this book.

QUESTIONS TO GUIDE E-PORTFOLIO PREPARATION

1. Which of your artifacts might be included in an e-portfolio that are impossible to present in a traditional paper portfolio in a binder?

2. Are the artifacts you listed above in digital form? What will you need to do in order to convert nondigitized files to a digital format?

3. What software is available for you to use in the preparation of an e-portfolio? Which are you required (or have you opted) to use? What are the advantages and disadvantages of this choice?

7

PowerPoint Basics

Focus Questions

- What is the structure of a PowerPoint presentation?
- Does copyright law affect the PowerPoint presentation author?
- How can graphics, music, and video clips be added to PowerPoint?
- Can PowerPoint "link" to documents that are already written?

❖ INTRODUCTION

This chapter will describe the production of a high-quality PowerPoint presentation, including graphics, music, and links to Web resources. This chapter uses a more traditional linear presentation so as to familiarize the e-portfolio author with the PowerPoint pull-down menus, shortcuts, and toolbars. The chapter will be presented using its common Office 2003 look. Special notes are included to outline the differences in a variety of PowerPoint features when using MS Office 2007 and the Mac OSX operating system. The MS Office 2007 version is greatly enhanced from its 2003 version, but its features are fully realized when running on the Vista operating system. It is, however, beyond the scope of this text to present a comprehensive Vista users' manual, so the notes about PowerPoint 2007 will be limited to those

Refer to the
Microsoft
PowerPoint
2007
Screenshots
on the
Student
Resource CD

features discussed in detail using the PowerPoint 2003 version and running Windows XP. The text uses a number of "screenshots" based on PowerPoint 2003, but the CD that accompanies this text holds a file of parallel screenshots based on PowerPoint 2007. This chapter is not, in and of itself, intended to enable the production of an e-portfolio but is, rather, a guide to the more common uses of the program called PowerPoint. Adapting the program to use as an e-portfolio development tool will be the subject of subsequent chapters.

❖ START AT THE BEGINNING

Refer to the
Student
Resource CD
to see the
ABCDEF
portfolio
example

Before starting the PowerPoint construction process, you should know what you would like to do. Doing an outline of the content of your presentation is an excellent way to begin planning your presentation. Drawing a "map" of your presentation will augment that outline and serve as detailed planning for what you plan to present. In Chapter 6, a linear presentation was mapped in Figure 6.2. We will use that presentation within this chapter to demonstrate the basic characteristics of PowerPoint. An example of this kind of presentation is the low-tech teacher preparation e-portfolio of student "Abcdef," which is included as a linear presentation on the CD accompanying this text.

Refer to the
Student
Resource CD
for a sample
storyboard

For any presentation, planning the presentation is key. Using an outline or storyboard approach, plan the presentation and the content you wish to provide. A storyboard would use a series of text boxes in a word processor, note cards, or even pieces of paper on which the content of every slide would be planned. The plan would begin by identifying the requirements of the standards to be used, what a reflection might contain for each of the standards, and which of many artifacts you might choose to include in the presentation. You should create a text box for each slide and move the text box as the presentation grows. If note cards are prepared for all of this content, it is then possible to order the cards as you would like to have the presentation slides ordered. In that this first attempt at using PowerPoint is a linear presentation, it will be developed using the presentation software in the same way as the note cards might be revealed to a viewer—a linear approach moving from one slide to the next slide. Given, then, that the planning for the presentation is complete and fits into a format reflected in Figure 6.2, we will begin by starting up the application.

❖ STARTING POWERPOINT

In both the Windows (on an IBM computer or clone) and Macintosh platforms, the exact manner of starting PowerPoint depends on the display option that is showing on your computer screen. In part determined by the operating system (OS), the differences are probably familiar to most people. All of the descriptions that follow may be altered through the use of shortcuts that may have been installed on your system to allow for a more efficient identification and start of programs you use more frequently. In most Windows systems, you would follow the instructions below:

- Click on "Start" and select "All Programs."
- Click on "Microsoft Office." A pop-up box will present a number of options.
- Select "PowerPoint" or "Presentation."

This sequence of actions will start or launch the program, showing first a PowerPoint title page displaying the program name and the version you are using. The first widow on which you will work is a default title page for your presentation.

If you have a PowerPoint presentation written or if you are working on a presentation that has been saved at some point in its development, you would click on the pull-down "File" menu and select "Open." You will be faced with the need to identify the presentation through the familiar "Browse" command in the Windows environment or the Macintosh listing of saved files. You would select the filename that represents the presentation you wish to open, and PowerPoint should open it. A note is warranted in that a newer version of PowerPoint will probably be able to open a presentation written in an older version of PowerPoint, but the opposite may not work due to a number of new features that may have been used. It is also notable that a presentation file composed in the Windows environment will open on a Macintosh, *but a presentation composed on a Macintosh will not automatically run in the Windows environment.* The Macintosh user may have to save and provide the extension ".ppt" to the end of the filename for a Macintosh-composed presentation to run in Windows. It is noted that Mac-OSX may add the extension automatically. This process should also underscore the importance of naming your presentation files carefully so that you are able to recognize them easily.

PowerPoint 2007 Note:

Opening a preexisting presentation file will require you to click on the Office Icon (by default, in the upper-left corner of the window) and select "Open." Browsing and selection are the same as in Office 2003.

It is recommended that you now type in the title of the presentation and the subtitle or author information in the second (subordinate) text box on the default title slide. This provides information that will display and provide you with some idea of the look of the presentation as you go through the step of applying a design template for color background. As is the practice in any computer work, depending on your typing ability, the care and time taken to enter information on each slide, and your comfort level, the presentation should be saved frequently. Follow these instructions for saving:

- Click on the "File" pull-down menu.
- Pull down and click on "Save As" (to establish a presentation filename) OR
- Click on "Save" in order to update a previously named presentation file.

PowerPoint 2007 Note:

PowerPoint 2007 saves presentations with the extension .pptx, which is not compatible with earlier PowerPoint versions looking for an extension .ppt. Therefore, until PowerPoint 2007 becomes the standard, during the saving process, save the PowerPoint 2007 file as if it were prepared in PowerPoint 2003. Select the Office Icon and then "Save As." You will have to choose to save the file as the default "PowerPoint Presentation" (.pptx) or as a "PowerPoint 1997–2003" (.ppt) file in the pop-up window.

❖ SELECTING A SLIDE BACKGROUND

When you start PowerPoint, the "normal" view is the default manner in which the information is displayed. The selected slide (the one on which you are working) occupies a central position with either a content outline or representation of the slides in the presentation (the choice being elected from tabs at the top of the column) being on the left side of the selected slide.

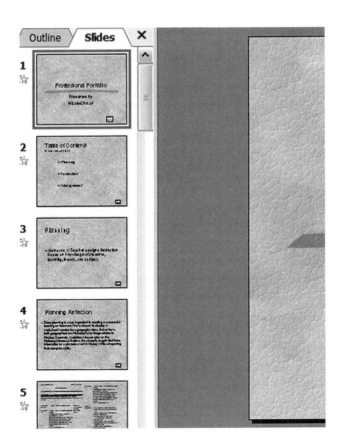

To the right of the selected slide is another column of information. It is called the task pane and will be headed with "Getting Started" at start-up. Click on the arrow to the right and select "Slide Design" from the drop-down menu for a template that will add color and arrangement. From the arrow to the right of the "Slide Design" heading, a number of other options are available from the task pane. This includes a shortcut to beginning a new presentation. Clicking on "Slide Design" and activating "New Presentation" will allow you to use either a blank presentation or a design template presentation (the default option), apply a slide design first, or use the auto-content wizard. The auto-content wizard will automatically set up a basic presentation based on input information. Most users are comfortable with the design template option for new presentations.

PowerPoint 2007 Note:

The command for adding a new slide is found under the "Home" tab, as is the pop-up window that allows for the definition of the specific slide design.

Continuing with your presentation from your title slide requires that you select the slide design template you wish to use. You can examine the options for a background that are displayed for that purpose. For e-portfolios, the background should be fairly neutral so as not to detract from the presentation of the reflections and artifacts. Pastels or darker solids with no or very subtle patterns work well. Among the presentation designs are a number of low-impact designs such as "beam" and "textured." For other kinds of presentations, a number of more eye-catching designs are available, ranging from "profile" to "fireworks" patterns. An additional number of presentation templates are available to allow for designs that can facilitate quite a few specialized presentations, many of them business oriented. You may also elect to import design templates from the Microsoft Office online Web site by clicking on that option at the end of the design template options to the right of the title slide. It is important to reemphasize that the wrong background can detract from a good presentation. Consider the purpose of your presentation, and then select the background that is appropriate.

PowerPoint 2007 Note:

Slide backgrounds are available from the "Design" tab. Available designs are displayed as you browse the selections.

As you add slides to your presentation, the number of different slide layouts from which you can choose is fairly large but can be summarized as title, bulleted lists, bulleted lists with graphics, charts, graphs, and blank pages with and without titles. The type of slide that you choose to use is defined by the type of information that you wish to place into the slide. Once you have completed putting information into the title slide, you select the next slide simply by using "Insert" and "New Slide" from the pull-down menu or, if you prefer, you can

Refer to the
Student
Resource CD
for a sample
storyboard

select the icon from the toolbar that consists of a page with a "glint" of light (under the "Home" tab in PowerPoint 2007). Either will display slide layout options to the right of the selected slide. Note that instead of being titled "Slide Design," the right column is headed with "Slide Template." The sequence of slides that will be selected here will be consistent with the sequence required for the presentation outlined in the storyboard that is part of the CD accompanying this text. The sample presentation would first have a title page and then a bulleted list containing Standard 1. A third slide would then be selected as a bulleted list and contain the information labeled as *reflection*. It is important to note that as information is put onto the slide, the program will accept another item of information, which can be formatted to be preceded by a bullet whenever the "Return" key is pressed.

When placing information in the form of a bulleted list, items can be placed below the bulleted item and shown in a subordinate position by using the "Tab" key to indent the bullet. This allows for an "outline-like" look to the list. The template design will determine the type of bullet that will change for the subordinate item. If you are constructing a bulleted list and want a subordinate item to be moved to a superior position, holding "Shift" while using "Tab" will allow the indentation to be reversed. Even the type of bullet can be changed within the "Format" pull-down menu.

PowerPoint 2007 Note:

Font adjustments in PowerPoint 2007 are made under the "Home" tab, with font definition and size in the font section and bullet options in the paragraph section.

❖   SELECTION OF FONT TYPE AND SIZE

The choice of font is, perhaps, as important to consider as the type of background being used. Serif fonts are those that have "decorations" on the ends of each "stroke" of the letter. The font named "Times New Roman" is a serif font. The capital "T" used at the beginning of the sentence has decorations on the bottom of its base and at the ends of the bar forming the cross at the top of the "T." Especially when projecting these letters, the serif decorations may make the words of the presentation difficult to read. When selecting font type, consider that a *readable* font is desirable, and these are most often found among the sans serif fonts. Examples of sans serif fonts are Arial, Chicago, and Helvetica. The comic-strip appearance of the font "comic sans," which is very popular in many instructional applications, is probably not appropriate for a presentation of a professional portfolio. It is always best to stay with the font selected throughout the presentation.

Altering the size and color of any information placed onto a slide is possible by using the options under the "Format" pull-down menu or the appropriate icons from the formatting tool bar. Ordinarily, if the presentation is being projected, no font size smaller than 24 point should be used. As the e-portfolio is not going to be projected in most circumstances, smaller font sizes may be used with appropriate attention being given to the needs of the viewer. The font size and style are also displayed and can be altered in the formatting toolbar. Toolbars can be viewed or hidden from the "View" pull-down menu.

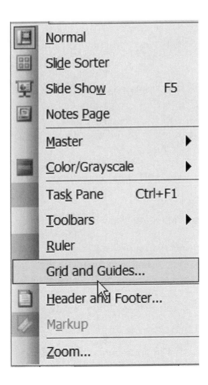

❖ SELECTING SLIDE VIEWS TO ACCOMPLISH WORK

The menu item called "View" is important to review at this point. The sequence that is discussed thus far should look like Figure 7.1. The order of the slides is evident in the "Normal" view, which is the view in which slides are created and edited. In the "Normal" view, a presentation is opened by the default setting, and it is in this view that most work will be accomplished. It will show the basic slide setup, including the text boxes into which information and/or graphics are normally placed. The text boxes define the regions most often used to contain information and the font size most often used for that information. It is possible to

Figure 7.1   Sequence for Creating a Basic PowerPoint Presentation

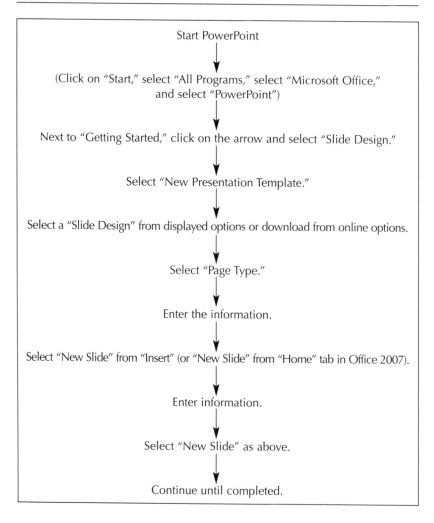

Mac OSX Note:

To start PowerPoint, double-click on the Microsoft Office X icon in the applications folder in the hard drive, and then double click on the PowerPoint program. Although you may elect to use the auto-content wizard, it is recommended you click on "PowerPoint Presentation." Chose the title slide layout, and under the "Format" pull-down menu, select "Slide Design" and select an appropriate background appearance. Enter information and add slides as in the Office 2003 environment.

PowerPoint 2007 Note:

There is no task pane, but operations within PowerPoint 2007 are initiated simply by selecting the appropriate tab.

---

highlight and change font sizes and color, as well as click on the borders and corners of the text boxes to change both their location and size.

The "Slide Sorter" view will show the order in which the slides are arranged. The slides are numbered and displayed in miniature in the order that they are currently arranged. As a presentation is written, the slides are added to the end of the presentation, and they are numbered reflecting that addition. It is possible to click on a slide at any point in the presentation and insert a new slide at that point. The program will make room for the slide and automatically renumber the new and subsequent slides. You can also change the position of an existing slide within a presentation. Clicking on and holding (dragging) a slide will enable you to move its position. Any changes made within this view will be reflected in the order and the numbering displayed by the view and will change the order in which the slides are revealed in the slide show.

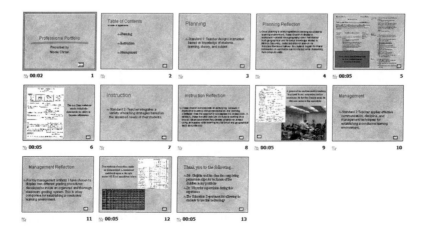

A good PowerPoint presentation is one in which the speaker does not simply read the slides to the audience. Reading the slides of a PowerPoint presentation is one of the most serious errors made in the use of a potentially powerful presentation tool. It is nearly certain that everyone has heard, or felt, the following emotional response to such a presentation: "I could have understood this information better had it been simply mailed to me." The "Notes" view can allow a presenter to avoid this error by creating speaking notes on the lower half of a printed page while showing the associated slide on the top half of the page. The speaking notes are entered and saved as a part of the presentation file but show only in the "Notes" view, which can be printed. The notes do not show in any other view and are not included in the projected slide show. As a planning and preparation format, however, this view is invaluable.

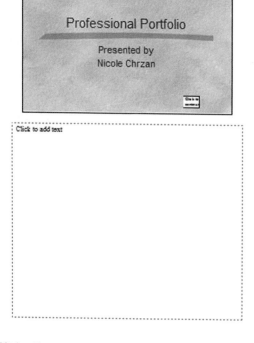

The "Slide Show" view triggers the PowerPoint show, and the escape key will stop the show. When the escape key is pressed, the last viewed slide is thrown into the Slide View. The slide can then be edited in this view. It is common during the preparation phase of a presentation to find and correct an error by using the escape key.

Once a show has been stopped, the Slide Show command will start the presentation on Slide 1. While the presentation is running, a small, somewhat camouflaged control panel is available at the bottom-left corner of the slide. It is a box containing a left and right arrow, a slanted pen, and a PowerPoint slide icon. Clicking on the slide icon will reveal a navigation tool to move to the next slide or to another slide by number or title, or to end the show. The arrows allow you to move forward or backward. The pen will allow you to designate a pointer or a pen to be used during the show (controlled by the mouse). If you start a show and wish to go immediately to a slide—perhaps the fifth slide in the order of the presentation, called "Standard 2"—the use of this small control panel will allow you to do this.

PowerPoint 2007 Note:

Under the "Slide Show" tab, the presentation can be started with the option of showing the presentation from the beginning or from the current slide. Although the camouflaged control panel is not evident, pointing to the lower left of the slide show will cue the expected features, including "Go to Slide" and "Pointer" options. The "View" options discussed below are not available at the lower left of the slide in PowerPoint 2007 but can be selected from the "View" tab.

The same choices that are available under the pull-down menu called "View" are available from small icons in the lower-left corner of the PowerPoint slide work area in every view, except "Slide Show." The icon that represents a page on which a line is drawn is for the "Slide" view. The matrix of four boxes represents four different slides in the "Slide Sorter" view. The box on top of a vertical line represents a projection screen and will activate the "Slide Show" view. Clicking on these small icons is no different from selecting the option under "View" in the pull-down menu, but it may be quicker.

The "Slide Show" pull-down menu has a number of special effects that can be used to put finishing touches on a PowerPoint slide show. If the presentation in Figure 7.1 is completed, activating "Slide Show" will allow the presentation to move from slide to slide, with all contents of each slide immediately replaced by the contents of a subsequent slide upon a mouse click. Suddenly revealing information from one slide to the next may not be the best use of PowerPoint. To make the presentation more effective, you can reveal information one piece at a time. First, slides may be set to change from one to the next using sophisticated effects that are not unlike transitions seen in video productions. This is called "Slide Transition" and can be established by following these steps:

- Select the "Slide Show" pull-down menu.
- Select "Slide Transition" or select from the arrow at the top right of the task pane.
- Select an "effect" from the list of possible effects.
- Select the speed of the transition effect: fast, medium, or slow.
- Select whether or not the effect should be accompanied by sound.
- Select whether the transition should occur with a mouse click or automatically.
- Select whether the effect should be applied to the selected slide or to all slides.

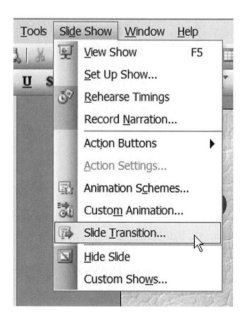

Again, the decision to use any of these options needs to be derived by considering whether the effect adds to or detracts from the purpose of the slide show.

Another effect available under the "Slide Show" pull-down menu is animation. Animation allows for the contents of a slide to be revealed one piece at a time during the slide show. Even "back in the day," when the overhead projector was a modern technology, the contents of a transparency were often "masked" with a piece of paper that was pulled down when it was appropriate to expose the contents of the transparency. A similar effect is possible in PowerPoint to reveal slide contents one piece at a time. Select "Custom Animation" from under the "Slide Show" pull-down menu or select "Custom Animation" from the task pane using the arrow at the top-right corner. A bulleted list, for example, can be set to reveal one bullet at a time and even reveal subordinate bullets each in turn under the major bullet in an outline situation. If graphics or music are used, custom animation will allow for those features also to be revealed in the presentation just at the correct moment, either automatically or with a mouse click. In the normal view, select a text box, graphic, or music symbol and use the task pane. Custom animation is accomplished using effects similar to the slide transition options by following the steps discussed previously.

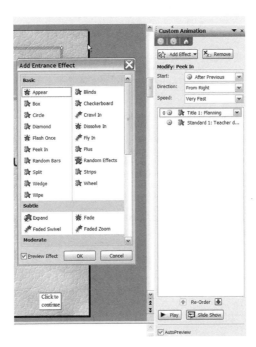

Figure 7.2   Sequence for Adding Slide Transition and Animation

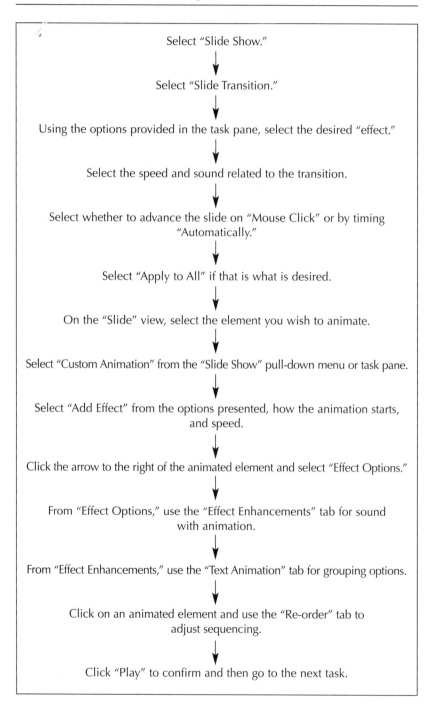

Select "Slide Show."

↓

Select "Slide Transition."

↓

Using the options provided in the task pane, select the desired "effect."

↓

Select the speed and sound related to the transition.

↓

Select whether to advance the slide on "Mouse Click" or by timing "Automatically."

↓

Select "Apply to All" if that is what is desired.

↓

On the "Slide" view, select the element you wish to animate.

↓

Select "Custom Animation" from the "Slide Show" pull-down menu or task pane.

↓

Select "Add Effect" from the options presented, how the animation starts, and speed.

↓

Click the arrow to the right of the animated element and select "Effect Options."

↓

From "Effect Options," use the "Effect Enhancements" tab for sound with animation.

↓

From "Effect Enhancements," use the "Text Animation" tab for grouping options.

↓

Click on an animated element and use the "Re-order" tab to adjust sequencing.

↓

Click "Play" to confirm and then go to the next task.

Mac OSX Note:

Animation and transition are found under the "Slide Show" pull-down menu. Slide transition is established from a single dialog box. The custom animation dialog box uses an effects tab to specify the effects and sound, an order and timing tab to determine the animation order and option of mouse click or timing for animation start, and an options tab for grouping text entry by levels (of subordinate text).

PowerPoint 2007 Note:

The animation and transition options discussed above are all available in PowerPoint 2007 under the "Animations" tab. Slide transition is available from a section called "Transition to this slide," and the "Animation" section contains animation and custom animation. Controlling how the animation/transition is triggered (click or automatic) is available as the animation or transition is defined.

- Select the "Custom Animation" task pane.
- From the "Normal" view, select the feature (title, object, or text) to be animated.
- Select "Add Effect" from the task pane and select "Entrance or Other Option."
- Select the animation effect to be added.
- Each feature to be animated will appear in the order of animation below the effect.
- Use the drop-down arrow to the right of an animated element for options and timing.
- Repeat for each feature of the slide to be animated.
- Click on an animated element and use arrows at the bottom of the task pane to reorder.
- To add sound to animation, use the drop-down arrow to the right of the element.
- Select "Effect Options" and "Effect Enhancements," and select sound from the drop-down menu.
- To animate subordinate points in a bulleted list, select "Effect Options" as above.
- Select the "Text Animation" tab, and use the "Group Text" options appropriately.
- Select "Play" to preview or move on to the next slide.

❖ A WORD ABOUT COPYRIGHT LAW

Before discussing how to add images, sound, and movies to a presentation, it is necessary to discuss how the law may be a limiting factor. The law regarding the use of material from the Internet is not very clear at the present time. The Digital Millennium Copyright Act (DMCA) of 1998 (P.L. 105-304) established restrictions on the use of such material that are very strict. One business affected by this law was Napster, a Web site very popular in the late 1990s and into 2000. With Napster, music lovers could avoid retail prices by downloading music free from the Internet. Although it was not the only such site, by 2000, the DCMA had forced Napster to change its operations to allow for the remuneration of the artists. As of this writing, the final court decision regarding (and pending the sale of) Napster is not known.

Less sinister than avoiding retail pricing is the use of Web-based materials for educational and research purposes. Although these are purposes for which "fair use" would apply to print materials, there was no such allowance for electronic materials until recently. The November 2002 passage of the Technology Education and Copyright Harmonization Act (TEACH [sic]) reduced the strictness of the DMCA by excluding college instructors' use of portions of dramatic works, even when they are part of an online course ("College Media Group," 2003). However, in establishing some level of the use of copyrighted material, TEACH is in opposition to DMCA. It seems clear that federal law is not speaking with one voice when it comes to the protection of materials made available through the Internet. A great deal of effort is being invested in developing specific policies regarding intellectual property. Where does that leave an electronic portfolio developer who wishes to use material from the Internet as part of the e-portfolio?

❖ IS THERE FAIR USE?

The answer is not easy, and the following presents guidelines that are general in nature. In no way do we purport to be copyright lawyers. Furthermore, we urge that if there is a question at all, the specifics should be referred to a qualified copyright lawyer. Before using any images or textual information from the Internet, a user is advised to become familiar with and make decisions regarding the particular material being considered for use within the context of the portfolio being developed. How is a decision reached? Copyright issues regarding

Internet resources are exceedingly complex, as can be seen on one particularly good Web site (see the UT Web site at www.utsystem.edu/ OGCIntellectualProperty/COPYPOL2.HTM). There are no clearly identifiable or easily summarized rules that guide the decision as to protection. For the purposes of this text, we shall focus on the same four questions that guide fair use decisions for traditional copyright issues (Amen, Keogh, & Wolff, 2002) as the basis for the decision-making process. Although these four questions are traditionally applied to print materials, it seems that these questions may also be somewhat applicable to the digital era. It cannot be ignored that there is an increase in attention to the profit motive in Internet resources as compared to traditional materials, but the following may serve to illustrate that the four questions could still be appropriate.

Question 1: What is the "purpose and character" of the use? In terms of an e-portfolio, this question seeks to determine if the product serves an educational or a commercial purpose. If the use of the e-portfolio is more educational and less commercial, then the fair use standard of this question is more closely met. If the purpose of the e-portfolio is a moneymaking commercial enterprise, then the fair use standard of this question is not met. An example of the former would be an e-portfolio on which a photograph of a university building is used when illustrating an exit portfolio of a student from a program of that university. The photograph is taken from the university Web site containing many images and does not represent an opportunity for the student to market the photo as part of a commercial purpose (selling T-shirts, for example). This use of the photo as described seems to be compliant with the first standard. In contrast would be an image of a university building as part of a Web site forecasting the arrival of a particular fast-food restaurant close to the university but independent of it. The photograph then becomes a part of a commercial enterprise by advertising the restaurant, possibly suggesting a linkage between the two entities, and thus does not meet this first standard.

Question 2: What is the nature of the work? In general terms, the more factual and widespread the information might be, the more it meets this standard for fair use. In contrast, the more creative and less known the information might be, the less the material would meet this standard of fair use. Returning to the examples used previously, a photograph of a building could reasonably be taken by anyone with a camera—that is, the work may not necessarily be very creative. Neither does the photo contain "secret" material, as most buildings on most campuses are well known. As described, the photograph seems to meet this second standard. On the other hand, if the photograph of the building actually represented an architect's concept as part of a "bid" to build a new student union building, then the nature of the work is both creative and somewhat secret. The photograph, in this case, would not meet the second standard referring to the "nature of the work."

Question 3: How much of the copyrighted work is being used? This standard seeks to identify the volume of material being used relative to the total amount of material. This standard of fair use is met if the work being used is but a small portion that does not represent a significant use of the total work. One source cites a general rule for significant use as 10% or less of the total work (see the NC Schools Web site at www .ncpublicschools.org/copyright1.html). If the work being used does represent a greater portion of the total work, then this standard of fair use is not met. Again, drawing on the photographic material referred to earlier, the photograph of the university building is just a small segment of the university Web site that features much more information as well as many more photographs. The use of a single photograph is not a significant portion of the work and seems to meet the fair use standard of this question. On the other hand, the future student union building may be the only substantial part of a university or of an architect's Web page announcing the award of the bid for construction of that building. Because the image of the building is the major part of the work, this example does not meet the fair use standard of this question.

Question 4: What is the effect on the market for the use of the work? The intent of this question is to identify if there could be lost revenue as the result of the use of the work. Referring to the photographs used earlier, the case may hinge on issues of economics—was money lost by the owner of the materials, or was money made with the image by persons other than the owner of the material? The use of the image of the university building does not necessarily "cost" the university anything in terms of lost revenue. Given the wide recognition of university buildings, a photograph of one does not seem to be a threat to the university's expectations. However, a particular restaurant's use of an image that is an architect's rendering of a student union may cost the university money when competing restaurants do not bid on vending space because it appears that a deal has been made. The former seems to meet, whereas the latter does not seem to meet, the standard of the fourth question guiding the decision of fair use.

Allow one further disclaimer. We are not lawyers, and arguments to the contrary could be made of each of the examples provided above. As Amen et al. (2002) pointed out in reference to print materials, "These guidelines, which govern fair use decisions, were recognized as part of the law. However, enshrining fair use guidelines . . . has not by any means made deciding fair use clear-cut. Plenty of room remains for interpretation" (p. 22). Furthermore, the use of material for a presentation should be subject to the same standards of citation as would material from print sources. The common bibliographic citation systems (including those of the American Psychological Association and the Modern Language Association of America), as well as other standard documentation formats, have established rules and models of citation and referencing of electronic materials. Documentation and a list of references should be expected in an electronic presentation, as is the case with any use of print material. In any event, the use of copyrighted materials from any source at any level, without appropriate documentation of their source, is a form of plagiarism that cannot be tolerated.

❖ ADDING CLIP ART TO THE PRESENTATION

PowerPoint has a number of clip art graphics available for use within the program's built-in library. Selecting a bulleted list with a graphics icon is one way to ensure that there is room for clip art to be inserted. Follow these steps for clip art internal to the program:

- Click on "Insert" pull-down menu.
- Click and hold on "Picture."
- Select "Clip Art."
- Select "Category."
- Click "Insert" button.

Follow these steps for clip art external to the program and saved on some media:

- Click on "Insert" pull-down menu.
- Click and hold on "Picture."
- Select "From File."
- Browse to identify the source of the image.
- Identify the specific image.
- Click "Insert" button.

Clip art saved in most common formats (TIF and EPS) is available to be used within PowerPoint presentations.

When graphics are being pulled from a file outside of the clip art library, the images may need to be sized to fit the space reserved for their use. This resizing can be accomplished by clicking on and moving the "handles" located on the edges and corners of the graphics box. The handles on the edges will move only the dimension described by that edge, and the corner will move both dimensions described by that corner. Moving the handle on the left edge will only permit the left edge to be moved closer to or further away from the right edge. Clicking on and holding the upper-right corner will move both the upper edge toward the lower edge and the right edge toward the left edge. Moving the upper-right corner handle will cause them both to move in a proportional manner. Moving the entire image is possible by clicking on the image and dragging it in the direction you want it to move. This could be necessary previous to any resizing, for the image may be imported in a manner too large to see the side and corner handles. You would need to drag the entire image in a single direction, perhaps several times, to find the edges and corners.

PowerPoint 2007 Note:

Clip art and pictures may be added to a presentation from the "Insert" tab.

❖ ADDING INTERNET IMAGES TO THE PRESENTATION

Some graphics that you would like to use may be located on the Internet. Several popular sites contain tremendous collections of clip art offered for free use. They are easy to use and fairly self-explanatory. Many of the sites you may "hit" in a "free clip art" Web search are soliciting your subscription for a larger service. So, as always, be careful what you are doing if information is required to download clip art images.

Graphics on the Internet, however, are not limited to clip art. Some graphics that you may wish to use are images that are drawings or pictures that are posted on Web sites. These may be copy-protected, and, if so, you might not be allowed to copy or save them. If a graphic posted to the Internet is copy-protected, it would be unethical and possibly illegal to try to download it, anyway. Even if you can download or copy an image, unless you are granted permission to use the images from the site, the use of the graphic should be accompanied by a citation much in the same way that you might cite a passage from another source in a paper.

Capturing a graphic from the Internet is actually quite easy in most cases (see Figure 7.3). The most difficult aspect of using Internet graphics is actually locating the graphic you might want to use. In most cases, you would start your Internet browser and do a search for whatever you are looking for. Images of virtually anything can be found: from pictures of apples to the color patterns of a zebra, from pictures of the Grand Canyon to images of alien autopsies. Because this resource is huge and largely unpoliced, the problems with validity need to be considered from the same perspectives as when considering the validity of Web-based information in other forms of research. Follow these steps to capture an Internet graphic.

Windows environment:

- From your Web browser, find the graphic of interest.
- Right click on the graphic.
- Select "Save Image to File."
- Name the file so that it is recognizable.
- Return to PowerPoint.
- Insert as discussed earlier as a graphic external to the program.

Macintosh environment:

- From your Web browser, find the graphic of interest.
- Click and hold for a pop-up menu.
- Select "Save Image . . . "as described above or "Copy Image" depending on OS version.
- Return to PowerPoint.
- Select the slide on which the image should be located.
- Click on "Paste Special" if image is copied under the "Edit" pull-down menu.
- Insert a saved image as described above if "Save Image . . . " was used.

Figure 7.3   Adding Web Images to the Presentation

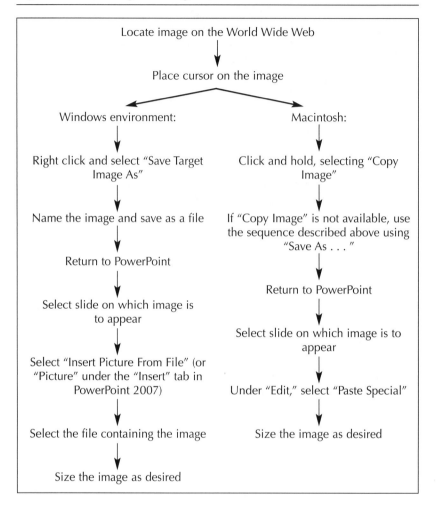

❖ ADDING SOUND TO THE PRESENTATION

A PowerPoint presentation may be augmented by music in several different ways. The PowerPoint program does come preloaded with some sound files. They can be accessed as follows:

- Click on "Insert" in the pull-down menu (or the "Insert" tab in PowerPoint 2007).
- Click on "Movies and Sound."
- Choose "Gallery."

It is possible to select from those files that are part of the program, and it is very easy to download additional sound clips from the Internet. However, there are many other ways to insert sound. The kinds of sound files that can be added to a PowerPoint presentation are somewhat limited as compared to a number of other programs that can be used for the construction of e-portfolios, but unless you are creating an e-portfolio as a music composer, the limitation is not a serious obstacle.

Both the Macintosh and Windows platforms are now usually preloaded with programs to permit a portfolio author to record his or her own audio files. Using nothing more than an inexpensive microphone, soundover and narration can be added to a PowerPoint presentation. In the Windows environment, the sound recorder is located within the accessories section of the Start menu. The default for saving audio files by recording (also called *capturing audio*) is a WAV file, a format that is compatible with PowerPoint. Follow these steps to record sound using the PowerPoint program rather than the OS:

- Click on "Insert."
- Click and hold on "Movies and Sound."
- Select "Record Sound."
- Identify the sound input device.
- Name the file, and select the red button to begin recording.
- The blue square will stop the recording, and the blue arrow will play the recording.
- Click "OK" to insert the sound.

Sound files can also be downloaded from the Internet. The common formats that can be used with PowerPoint include MIDI (musical instrument digital interface), WAV (waveform sound for Microsoft Windows), and MP3 (MPEG-1 Audio Layer-3). The more current versions of PowerPoint can also use ALF and ALFF files (common in the Macintosh environment) as well as a number of other, less frequently used file formats. Even using just the three major sound formats, it is possible to add anything that may be needed to augment a good PowerPoint presentation. Finding the appropriate file is the challenge in attaching an audio file to the PowerPoint presentation. Right click on the sound file on the Internet and "Save Target" as an easily identified filename. In the Mac OSX environment, click and hold for a pop-up menu to allow you to "Save Target" as a file. Then follow the steps cited above to add sound from a file. Caution is advised here in that sound and/or music files in excess of 100 kb, as well as movie (video) files of the same size, are saved as linked files (hyperlinked to an external file containing the sound or music). Only relatively small music, sound, and/or video files are saved as embedded files. Embedded means that the sound and so forth become part of PowerPoint, where linked files must travel independently with PowerPoint as separate, distinct files. The limit for linked files can be increased, but performance of PowerPoint will be reduced. With this limitation overcome simply by taking the sound and other files along with PowerPoint, adding sound is actually very easy.

Yet another option is to augment a PowerPoint presentation with sound or music from specific tracks on a CD recording. The CD will have to be in a CD-ROM drive for this option to be used. If the e-portfolio is on CD, then a second CD drive will be necessary, or the selected CD tracks would have to be saved to the same CD that carries the e-portfolio. The steps to follow to add this feature are as follows:

- Click on "Insert."
- Click on "Movies and Sound."
- Choose "Play CD Audio Track."
- Identify beginning and ending tracks in the "Play CD Audio Track" dialog box.
- Check (by clicking) the box if the tracks are to loop.
- Click "OK" to accept.

An icon will be placed on the slide where sound is to begin. It will show as a small speaker. The use of a CD for music in a presentation is very useful, for example, when presentations about specific places or people are made. Playing the music of a country behind a presentation focusing on that country, for example, could add to the overall quality of the presentation. A warning made elsewhere in this chapter is worth repeating here: Ensure that the use of audio of any type does not detract from the presentation.

❖ ADDING MOVIES TO A PRESENTATION

The use of movie clips is also possible. Two options exist for this use within the PowerPoint program. These options are similar to two options discussed above using movie clips from a gallery or a file. In the same way as using sound from a gallery of clips, PowerPoint will allow the use of any clips provided by the PowerPoint program or clips downloaded from the Internet. Similar to a sound clip, a movie clip can be used from a file. The movie must be in digital format, such as that taken from a Web site or made with a digital video camera. Editing and digitizing video is discussed later in this book.

Inclusion of movies within PowerPoint is useful in cases when the interview, action, or survey of the video adds to the presentation. In a presentation about a coral reef, a video of an actual coral reef may add a dimension to a presentation that is usually limited to still photos. The now overused but necessary warning is repeated here: Use movies only if the movie adds more to, rather than detracts from, the content of the presentation.

PowerPoint 2007 Note:

Adding video clips, movies, and sound is an option available from the "Insert" tab.

❖ ADDING INTERNET OR DOCUMENT LINKS TO THE PRESENTATION

Some presentations may be enhanced by links to specific Web sites or documents that are already created. The presentation author should read the fair use guidelines because using an entire work from a Web site or document link may be contrary to copyright law. If it is decided that the link is indeed appropriate, then the construction of the link is a relatively simple sequence of commands. The easiest way to create a hyperlink is to mimic the manner with which we are all familiar of navigating around the Internet. That is, a word or phrase is placed into the presentation where the hyperlink is desired. To create the hyperlink, follow these steps:

- Click on "Insert" and select "Text Box."
- Type words that will be the anchor from which the hyperlink will be launched.
- Highlight the words just typed in.
- Click on the "Insert" pull-down menu and select "Hyperlink."
- Specify the URL of the Web page or browse to find the page or file location.
- Click "OK."

If you expect to link to a Web page during the presentation, it must be remembered that the computer on which the presentation is being made must also be linked to the Internet. This is necessary so that when the hyperlink is clicked, the computer can access the URL as directed. In addition, the destination for hyperlinked documents, called a *pathway*, should be entered carefully. A *full pathway* will specify a file by naming the computer, the drive in use, the source media, the folders, and then finally the filename. If the presentation is transported to another computer with a different name or that uses a different drive or naming convention for the presentation, the *full pathway* may be useless. Using the alternative, the *relative pathway*, the program looks for files by their unique names rather than by the specifically identified location of a full pathway. The use of the relative pathway can avoid many hyperlink errors.

The relative pathway is the default on most applications and most versions, but the files (PowerPoint and any documents or source media files) must be in the same folder. This is a critical need and is the source of much anxiety if this simple rule is ignored. Again, PowerPoint and all files to which the presentation will hyperlink must be in the same single file folder with no subfolders, subdirectories, or partitions of any type. Another source of hyperlinking error is filename length. Some versions of PowerPoint will attenuate to eight characters in a filename in a hyperlink that is longer than that eight-character limit. Thus, when the hyperlink is activated to show the file saved as Geography Of Russia.doc, the hyperlink may be looking for another file with an attenuated filename of Geograph.doc. Since the Geograph.doc cannot be found, the hyperlink will not work. Therefore, limit to an eight-character length any file to which hyperlinks may be desired.

When establishing hyperlinks, it is important to recall that not all file types are supported by PowerPoint. A good rule of thumb is that anything to which you might want to hyperlink ought to be in a Microsoft form. Microsoft Word, Access, Excel, and PowerPoint are all supported during presentations in the PowerPoint program. In this way, it may be somewhat easier to ensure that the document to which you hyperlink actually works during a PowerPoint presentation. These kinds of links would be useful, for example, to show specific forms that viewers might have to use during a presentation about those forms. During an opening lecture of a class, teachers may wish to link to documents that they created as part of course requirements to clearly convey the use of those documents. A part of the same window in which you would identify your link allows you to redefine the word or phrase used to activate the link.

PowerPoint 2007 Note:

The option to add a hyperlink is found under the "Insert" tab. In the pop-up box that appears, the type of hyperlink must be selected to link to an existing file or Web page, to a place in the document, to create a new document, or to an e-mail address. Browsing is the same as in PowerPoint 2003.

❖ USING ACTION BUTTONS

Some users of PowerPoint presentations may find it easier to use hyperlinks by creating an action button. An action button initiates the hyperlink in the same way as clicking on the word or phrase as described above, but the button next to the word or phrase would be clicked. To use this option, follow the steps below:

- Click on "Slide Show."
- Click on "Action Button."
- Select the type of button you would like to use.
- Select the location of the button using the crosshairs.
- Specify the purpose of the link.
- Adjust size using the button's graphics handles.
- Adjust button color by using "Fill Color."
- Label the button by clicking on it and typing as desired.

To establish the hyperlink, follow the steps below:

- Click on "Slide Show."
- Click on "Action Settings."
- Select the appropriate link type in the "Hyperlink to" dialog box.
- Click "OK" to accept.

Please note that the button will not work unless the presentation is actually being shown, and it is advisable to check that all links work before the presentation is shown.

Mac OSX note:

Due to an error in the coding of PowerPoint for the Mac OSX, hyperlinks will not be saved as being relative, and using buttons thus created will not work. If the look of buttons is desired, create labels inside the button, highlight the label, and hyperlink using the words rather than the button.

❖ SHOWING THE PRESENTATION

Showing a PowerPoint presentation is your opportunity to show your technological prowess as well as your knowledge about the subject of the presentation. To ensure that your prowess is highlighted, you should try your presentation well before making your actual presentation, using the same equipment each time. This will provide enough time for you to make changes or address technical difficulties. These could include the type of media on which the program is saved, a need to have the Internet "up and running," unintended or absent animation, or features such as music or video clips that are in formats not compatible with the hardware. Although some of these can be addressed quickly, others will require more attention than might be comfortable while in front of an audience.

Refer to the Student Resource CD for these sample port-folios

As an indicator of the ease with which PowerPoint can be mastered, students in schools are regularly being required to use the program. The that accompanies this book contains examples of both a third-grade student e-portfolio and a graduation project. The research needed to create the graduation project may be overshadowed by the features in the third-grade portfolio, but both are produced to meet standards set for the students' individual situations. There are many examples of progressive school districts that have been using technological means to address standards much longer than most colleges and universities. Even so, the quality of the presentations warrants reminders of some presentation tips introduced in an earlier discussion.

First, practice the presentation so that all required mouse clicks or timings are well known. At the time of the presentation, the presenter should boot the computer, the program, and the presentation without the projector being turned on. The audience may be more interested in the navigational techniques you use than what is happening. Although it is encouraged that PowerPoint be set up and that the presentation is activated under "View Show" and ready for the projector to be turned on, it may have to be done during the presentation. In either situation, the audience should not have to watch as you start the presentation. In every case, please remember that you should, as a presenter, know enough about the subject that the contents of each slide need not be read to the audience. A final suggestion is that if you expect notes to be taken about the presentation and copyright is not a question, please prepare a handout to enable that activity within a more structured manner. To create a handout containing the presentation, follow the steps on the next page:

- Click on "Print" under the "File" pull-down menu to see a printing pop-up window.
- Use the dialog box to specify PowerPoint as the program "presets."
- Some printers will go automatically to a PowerPoint printer window.
- Choose the format prompted by the label "Print What."
- Select "Handout" with "Notes" or "Slides" as alternatives.
- Select output as "Color," "Grayscale," or "Black and White."
- Select "Print" to begin the printing process.

Using these tips, an allotment of time, and the strategies discussed in this chapter, a quality presentation can be prepared.

PowerPoint 2007 Note:

A handout may be prepared in PowerPoint 2007 by using the "View" tab. Select the "Handout Master," select slides per page, and then send to the printer from the Office Icon in the upper left of the window.

SUMMARY

PowerPoint presentation software can be a very powerful tool to augment a formal presentation. The use of PowerPoint can allow for the stepwise revealing of information (animation) while moving from slide to slide in a professionally appearing manner (slide transition). A basic slide presentation can be upgraded with the addition of graphics from the clip art file, which can be found as part of the program or in a variety of other media, or as digital images from a scanner or a camera. Images can be easily downloaded from the Internet, and the addition of sound can be accomplished by using selected tracks from a CD or by inserting either downloaded files or files that the author records. Movie clips can be downloaded or inserted from digital video taken by the author. Although all of this is possible, you must consider whether the addition of video, sound, music, graphics, and animation enhances the presentation or becomes a distraction. Furthermore, it must always be remembered that copyright law that is both strict and punitive can affect digital presentations such as PowerPoint. With some practice in avoiding common pitfalls regarding the use of PowerPoint, authoring high-quality presentations can serve an important role in raising the professional appearance of presentations.

QUESTIONS TO GUIDE E-PORTFOLIO PREPARATION

1. In what class(es) have you used PowerPoint (or have you seen PowerPoint used) to make a presentation? Which features of PowerPoint were included in the presentation?

2. Describe the difference between inserting a clip art image and an image that you can obtain from an Internet site.

3. Describe the difference between inserting a sound file that you record and a sound file that you can obtain from the Internet.

4. Describe how to insert a digital picture saved as a .jpg file and how to insert a lesson plan written and saved in MS Word.

5. What are the limitations beyond which use of Internet material may not be fair use of the Web site author's material?

8

Building Nonlinear PowerPoint Portfolios

Focus Questions

- How can hyperlinking add value to e-portfolios?
- How can PhotoShop Elements be used to accomplish basic image editing?
- What programs can be used to accomplish quality sound editing?
- What programs can be used to accomplish quality digital video file editing?

❖ INTRODUCTION

In Chapter 7, the discussion centered on the use of PowerPoint in its most common form. The PowerPoint presentation is, most commonly, a sequence of slides containing information that is viewed in order, from a title slide through the sequence to the end of the presentation. It bears mention here that the term *PowerPoint presentation* refers to the file, not a method of instruction, lecture, or speech. A speaker does not do a "PowerPoint presentation" but rather uses a PowerPoint presentation to assist in communicating the information contained in the instruction, lecture, or speech. The linear sequence of most PowerPoint presentations, aside from being the most common use of the program, is also the most common way that we all learn to use the program. It is the way that we are used to seeing the program used to illustrate important points in a lecture, highlight important facts of a speech, and communicate salient facts in an instructional environment. In this role, PowerPoint is not much different from the older technology of the overhead projector.

In the era of the overhead projector, transparency after transparency was exposed on the stage of a projector in order to throw images onto a large screen. With information sometimes masked by a piece of paper to hide material not yet discussed, the parallel of this technology with PowerPoint is obvious. Making a long presentation using multiple transparencies does lead to the horror story of many presenters. The story centers on that time many of us remember when the transparencies were out of order during a particularly important presentation! It is hard to forget the embarrassment as we searched through the stack of transparencies to find the one we really wanted. PowerPoint solves this potential disaster in that the presentation, moving from slide to slide, is set ahead of time by the presentation author. However, the rigid format of PowerPoint in its linear design can be a detractor in the use of the program.

Consider an example that would involve a question asked that is answered on a future slide. Using PowerPoint in its more common use, the presenter needs to click on the tool in the lower-left corner of the presentation slide and select the appropriate page from the options that appear in a window. Compare that to the need to simply shuffle through the transparencies to select the one that contains information that can easily answer the question asked. The ability to easily shift from slide to slide in an order other than originally planned is both a strength and a weakness of the overhead projector. Although the example above demonstrates how shuffling can be used to easily answer an unexpected question, the horror story of mishandling slides returns to mind.

One can also argue that the use of PowerPoint is warranted due to the ease of illustrating, animating, and adding other special effects to the presentation. In Chapter 7, adding special effects, illustrations, sound, and even movie clips is reviewed. These additional features, however, are added to the PowerPoint presentation only after the basic layout of the presentation is planned and entered on the slides of the presentation. Chapter 7 uses a storyboard approach to planning, but other types of planning (an outline format as an example) may be used. The need to plan the presentation is actually a strength of the technology, for without careful planning, the order and type of slides needed become as difficult to consider as the content of the presentation.

Other benefits of the PowerPoint presentation result from the time invested to create and save the presentation on media that allow an author to easily change information at any point in the future. Updating information contained on each slide is easy and does not require that slides be reprinted as they would have to be in a transparency-based augmentation of a speech using the overhead projector. With some minimal effort, a PowerPoint author can adjust colors, the slide sequence, and even the format of the slides. The trade-off for reaching the point when an author can realize the benefits of PowerPoint is the investment of time necessary to create the presentation ahead of the scheduled time of the instruction, speech, or lecture. Once the PowerPoint presentation is created, then the benefits can be enjoyed. What remains, then, is a discussion as to whether the PowerPoint program can be used to create an e-portfolio.

In the linear format, the PowerPoint program has an obvious limitation. A linear form of an e-portfolio is contained on the CD that accompanies this book. In this example, an author presents the standards and reflections in the work, followed by images of the candidate's performance that are also saved on slides contained within the presentation. For example, during an interview, the teacher candidate might provide a copy of the presentation for the convenience of the interviewer. But what Refer to the linear portfolios on the Student Resource CD would happen if the interviewer wants to see a particular piece of work that is toward the end of a presentation, or what if the only item of interest is a classroom management plan that is at the end of the presentation? The interviewer would have to know how to navigate using the window activated from the icon in the lower left of a slide during the slide show or would have to page through the presentation to the end. In a hardcopy portfolio, the interviewer would go to the index, find a page containing the particular piece of work of interest or the page containing the résumé, and skip directly to the pages of interest. Using the PowerPoint presentation in the more common format, the viewer is not easily able to go to random pages of interest. This chapter will focus on the use of PowerPoint in the construction of a nonlinear presentation through the creative use of the hyperlink, which can increase the ability of PowerPoint to be used in a less structured and less linear manner.

❖ MAKING POWERPOINT LESS LINEAR BY HYPERLINKING

The use of hyperlink was introduced in Chapter 7. This feature of PowerPoint can be used to link both within and outside of the presentation. Within the presentation, the hyperlink can be used to enable the program to move from one slide to another slide. The slide to which the hyperlink points can be the next slide, a previous slide, or a slide placed ahead of the next slide. The order of the slides then becomes more random based on which hyperlink is selected. Hyperlinks can be established to allow the slides to be viewed in an order that meets the need of an interviewer or of a viewer with a specific interest. In such a use, it is best to do this from an index that allows the easy identification of the slides that might be of interest to a person viewing the presentation. Two examples of such e-portfolios are on the CD accompanying this book in the Chapter 8 folder. They are by preservice teachers who are responding to a set of unit standards by preparing a program exit e-portfolio.

Refer to the nonlinear portfolios on the Student Resource CD

Using this organization in an e-portfolio, the preferences of the viewer are addressed. Perhaps the viewer is really interested only in the content contained on Slides 4 and 6. The use of hyperlinks within the program can make it possible to view only those slides. The order of the presentation could then be as follows: moving from Slide 1 (the title) to Slide 2 (the index), using the hyperlink to move ahead to Slide 4, hyperlinking back to Slide 2 (the index), hyperlinking ahead to Slide 6, and finally hyperlinking back to Slide 2 before ending the presentation. The presentation could also be viewed, using the hyperlinks, in the following order: Slide 1, Slide 2, Slide 6, Slide 2, Slide 4, and finally Slide 2. Hyperlinking from one slide to another slide within the presentation is called internal hyperlinking. Through the use of internal hyperlinking, the order of the slides selected for viewing is no longer a fixed sequence but is, rather, dependent on the needs or preferences of the viewer.

Hyperlinking to locations not a part of the presentation itself is called external hyperlinking. External hyperlinking can make a PowerPoint presentation even more rich by enabling quick linkages to a variety of files and even Internet sites. The use of the hyperlink can enable the viewer to "jump" from the PowerPoint presentation to word processing, database or spreadsheet documents, illustrations, or even sound or movie clips. This can be helpful to limit the size of the

PowerPoint presentation by making it unnecessary to include the external material within the presentation. It is also evident that if the material is already prepared in some format, it is unnecessary to duplicate the effort of copying and pasting, sizing, and formatting the information for inclusion in the presentation. Furthermore, the inclusion of a large amount of information in the actual presentation is in opposition to one of the primary rules that should guide the use of the presentation software—limiting the information to summary or important points only. The presentation should not include, for example, a lengthy report or extensive spreadsheet. However, if there is an interest in viewing these documents, hyperlinks can be written to "jump" to the file that contains these documents. An example used earlier might apply here. A presentation could be made as to when it is appropriate to use a specific business form, with a hyperlink to this form to be used only if necessary. As applied to the portfolio, the hyperlinks can be to samples of work from slides that are keyed to specific standards or requirements set for the portfolio. The manner in which hyperlinks can be created is outlined in Chapter 7.

The structure of nonlinear PowerPoint presentations can be further clarified by reviewing Figure 6.2 in Chapter 6, which shows an example of a presentation that includes three standards, four reflections, and four artifacts in a linear format. The viewer goes through the presentation in a more common way, from slide to slide, as the presenter or viewer clicks through the presentation. A nonlinear presentation is portrayed in Figure 6.3 (Chapter 6). This second nonlinear presentation features the same three standards, reflections, and four artifacts but enables the viewer to move randomly among the three standards, four reflections, and four artifacts. The viewer can choose the standards, reflections, and artifacts that are of interest. The viewer can navigate to and move among this information in a nonlinear manner by using hyperlinking to "jump" from slide to slide and access artifact files from appropriate reflections.

In Figure 8.1, the basic structure of the hyperlinked nonlinear PowerPoint presentation approaches the standard of an excellent e-portfolio. The difference between Figure 8.1 and Figure 6.3 is that the artifact files that are documents are linked to other files. MS Word documents can be hyperlinked much as PowerPoint can be. It can be accomplished either through the pull-down menu or from the icon on the toolbar. An example of the use of this "deep linking" would be possible using the example discussed earlier in the book. An e-portfolio could link to an MS Word document containing a new blank form that

Figure 8.1   Nonlinear Presentation Format That Will Run as a Normal Presentation Along the Dashed Line But That Can Use Hyperlinks to Become Less Linear Along Solid Lines

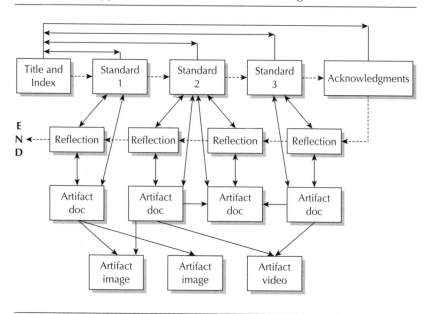

NOTE: This nonlinear presentation format will run as a normal presentation along the dashed line but can use hyperlinks to become less linear along solid lines. This model presents three standards with seven artifacts. Note that those artifacts that are documents can be hyperlinked, but image and video clips cannot be hyperlinked to other artifacts.

may be used in a business. That document could, in turn, be linked to a JPEG image of a completed (handwritten) form to illustrate a real business application of the form. Another example would be a hyperlink to a document containing a teacher's lesson plan that is, in turn, linked to a video clip of the lesson as it was taught.

The artifact files, separate from the presentation, will allow constant updating of the presentation simply by adding or removing hyperlinks to artifact files separate from the actual presentation. If a new spreadsheet project is better than an earlier one, a new hyperlink to the new file and the deletion of the old hyperlink will allow the updating of this particular artifact that might better meet a specific standard required in the e-portfolio. If a new lesson is taught and is more successful in practice than the earlier lesson, then this new sequence can be placed in an updated e-portfolio. The use of an index and the hyperlink feature of PowerPoint is absolutely essential in the process of creating a PowerPoint-based e-portfolio. It will, in fact, make the e-portfolio stand out from the ordinary "print and artifact" portfolios of earlier times.

❖ BUILDING A STRUCTURE FOR AN ELECTRONIC PORTFOLIO

The structure that is being suggested here is based on the experience and field testing of our efforts in the e-portfolio area. Several slides are absolutely necessary and include a title slide, an index slide, a slide for each standard, a slide for a reflection regarding how the selected artifacts meet each standard, and a slide of acknowledgments. The index will have links to slides of each standard. The slides of each standard will have hyperlinks back to the index (within the presentation) as well as hyperlinks to those artifacts that are selected for inclusion within the e-portfolio. It is clear that regardless of the purpose of the portfolio, there will be some content that is nonnegotiable and set by those requiring the e-portfolio. Regarding the majority of the portfolio content, it is recommended that e-portfolio authors be provided with some degree of freedom in selecting those artifacts that they think best define their mastery of a standard. Furthermore, the reflection should clarify what the standard means and how the artifact demonstrates that the standard is met. Thus, a structure of an e-portfolio will most closely resemble the diagram contained in Figure 8.1 as a nonlinear PowerPoint presentation.

Authoring the E-Portfolio

The first step in authoring an e-portfolio is selecting the standards that will be addressed. The specific structure of the e-portfolio will emerge from that decision. Careful planning will then occur with the portfolio author selecting those artifacts that are thought to most closely meet the requirements or standards. It is advisable to first carefully plan the presentation through the use of a pencil-and-paper top sketch—generally, the slide order and the links that will have to be made. Once the presentation is generally planned, collecting and digitizing the artifacts should occur first. It is highly recommended that all artifacts for the portfolio be collected in a single section within "My Documents" in the Windows environment, in a single file in the Macintosh environment, or on other removable media (flash drive or portable hard drive media).

As an e-portfolio author, you will be collecting a number of different types of files for use within the PowerPoint presentation and for objects outside of the presentation to which hyperlinks will point. Selecting these artifacts is the first challenge that you face, and the second will be saving these files in a digital format that can be easily accessed by the PowerPoint program. PowerPoint does not work equally well with all formats of files. It is recommended that the PowerPoint portfolio author convert files, as often as possible, to the equivalent file type produced by MS Word, Access, or Excel. Furthermore, it is recommended that the graphics files be converted, scanned, or photographed as JPEG images, and video should be saved in MPEG format. For many of these links, the use of QuickTime PictureViewer and QuickTime Player has increased the PowerPoint capability. Figure 8.2 lists common formats that have been used with the combination of QuickTime products and PowerPoint with no problem.

Converting files that are not compatible with PowerPoint is possible using "Save As" options or one of several programs designed to edit graphics and movie files. Examples of these programs include iMovie (on the Macintosh) and Adobe PhotoShop Elements. The files are opened, and using the "Save As" command, the file type can be changed to a new format. Altering the files to a readable file can be just that easy. It is important to make sure that all files are in a format that can be opened with a hyperlink from the PowerPoint program. Linking to a .gif image, for example, will probably result in a statement that the

Figure 8.2   Formats in Which Nondocument Artifact Files May Be Saved for Use With the PowerPoint Portfolio

Artifact type	Artifact formats
Graphic images	.emf, .gif, .jpeg, .png, .pict, .bmp, .rle, .dib
Video clips (movies)	.mpg, .mpeg, .mov, .wmf, .avi, .qt (quicktime)
Audio formats	.midi, .wav, .mp3

program was unable to open the image. A document that will not open is sure to interfere severely with a clear and fair assessment of an e-portfolio. Remember that the purpose of an e-portfolio is for it to be easily read by a viewer, and such technical glitches will complicate the task for the viewer and frustrate efforts to use the e-portfolio for whatever purpose is intended. Therefore, it is critical that the e-portfolio undergoes testing before its final submission.

As suggested earlier, it is recommended that all artifact files be saved to a specific folder. An alternative would be to save in-progress e-portfolio work in a partitioned space on a server to which access is controlled. The partition is a virtual "wall" defining a space that is accessible to only those who have authority to enter. Password protection of that space is an example of control. However, if the server is accessible by remote users, the potential of a problem is exacerbated. Security measures become necessary if there is the possibility that many people may be able to gain access to server space. This need for security is to ensure, as much as possible, that your files are not used by anyone else. Although there may be considerations related to copyright, there may also be ethical considerations. There are reasonable expectations that the images or examples used in a single e-portfolio will not be borrowed for publication in thousands of e-portfolios. It is important, then, to make sure your space on a server is partitioned and protected. Furthermore, it is important not to share the means of protection (e.g., tell others of your password). This may seem picayune, yet a great deal of work goes into your files, and they deserve a level of protection.

❖ EDITING IMAGES USING BASIC
    PHOTOSHOP ELEMENTS CAPABILITIES

Adobe PhotoShop is one of the most widely used graphics editors on the market. It is, unfortunately, relatively expensive. Fortunately, however, a scaled-down version of PhotoShop is available and is capable of doing all of those basic functions described below. The following comments and instructions are intended only to provide a very basic idea of the many capabilities of the PhotoShop Elements application. It is not intended that this be a manual for anything other than a few of the many features that are directly related to the production of well-done e-portfolios. The features that will be discussed are limited to the use of filters, cropping, editing images with brightness and color, and sizing. Other graphics editors are available as shareware or prepackaged with some computer purchases. However, Adobe's PhotoShop Elements is a valid alternative to the much higher priced (but more complete) full version of PhotoShop and is typical in terms of its operation. Any of these programs would be useful to beginning e-portfolio authors to correct some of the most common problems.

The use of images of individuals within your portfolio is a topic that has already been discussed. There is a need, moral and legal, to have releases from those persons who are included in your portfolio. A signed permission form is the only recommended way to proceed when obtaining this permission. Verbal permissions may be legally binding, but they are notoriously difficult to document. A sample letter and sample permission form are provided in Figure 8.3 and Figure 8.4, respectively. It is important that the permission form identifies the reason that the e-portfolio is being developed, the method and extent to which the e-portfolio will be shared, and the limits of the sharing. Although the actual signed statements are not necessary in the presentation, it is necessary to acknowledge the fact that the permissions have been received. What happens, however, if there is a feature in a slide or artifact that ought not be recognized? The image can be filtered. What if you want only part of the image? The image can be cropped. What if the light was too bright and the image is "washed out"? You can adjust for the brightness of the image. What if the image is too small or too large? You can resize the image. How these things are accomplished is the focus of the rest of this section.

Taking a Part of the Image: Cropping

Taking a part of an image is called *cropping*. An image that is to become part of an e-portfolio might simply have too much background to be effective in demonstrating the standard or requirement the image is to address. It is possible to decide what part of the image is important given the purpose for which it is selected and then to outline that region of the image. PhotoShop Elements allows the user to literally cut that portion of the image out of the rest of the image and to make a new image consisting of only that cut-out section. Cropping allows the portfolio author to direct a reader's focus to what is important. An image of a classroom in which the teacher is assisting a student may meet a standard, but the focus may not be obvious. The focus intended might be the teacher's individual helping. That could be emphasized by cutting out only that part of the picture showing the teacher and the student being helped while disposing of the rest of the class. A student's use of technology by using computerized lab interfacing during a chemistry experiment may be more important than other students working in groups at the same time. Cropping to limit the image to the student working with the experiment and the computer lab interfacing setup may provide a better artifact. Purging extraneous and possibly distracting portions of an image can strengthen an e-portfolio immensely.

Figure 8.3   Sample Cover Letter to Obtain Signatures on a Permissions Form

(Your name and your address here)

Insert date

Dear ("Person" whose image or material you wish to use)

As part of my (job search or professional requirements), I am completing an electronic portfolio for presentation to (prospective employers or to those interested in assessing my professional development). I am including many things within this portfolio, including samples of my work and other evidence that I meet (requirements or standards), which are the purpose of my portfolio development. All of this information is being saved in a digital form, and it is my intention to provide copies of the portfolio to those individuals who have a reason to view the portfolio. I may also use the portfolio for (large group presentations or any other use you might define).

I would like your permission to include (photos or other work), which (includes or identifies) you (as a focus of the photograph or as the source of work samples). I believe that this (photo or work) will contribute significantly to my ability to demonstrate that I meet the (requirements or standards) defined by the portfolio. If you have any questions, please feel free to call me at (your phone number here). If you would agree to provide permission, I would appreciate your completion and return of the attached permissions form in the attached postage-paid envelope.

Sincerely,

(Sign your name)

NOTE: The information within parentheses needs to be customized for your particular needs.

Figure 8.4   Sample Permission Form

Permission to use material

I am providing permission to (portfolio developer name here) to use material that (includes my image or my work—or that of my child) within an electronic portfolio that (portfolio developer name here) is developing. It is recognized that neither (my own or my child's) name will be used within the electronic portfolio. The portfolio will simply refer to the fact that all images or work belonging to other persons are used within the portfolio with permission.

The reason for the development of the portfolio is to (define the purpose here). Your (or your child's) image or work used within this portfolio still belongs to you (or your child) with all copyright and ownership rights. The portfolio will not be distributed as a commercial product, and confidentiality of all persons providing permission to use their work will be maintained to the fullest extent possible.

With this permission, I release (portfolio developer's name here) from liability that might arise from the inclusion of (my or my child's) (photo or work) within this portfolio.

_____

Print your child's name

_____   _____

Your signature   Date

_____

Print your name here

_____   _____

Address   Phone number

_____

_____

NOTE: The information within parentheses needs to be customized for your particular needs. "My or my child" and "your or your child" refer to the person providing permission for use of his or her material.

To crop an image, you must start PhotoShop Elements and then open the image. Follow the steps below to crop an image:

- Open PhotoShop Elements.
- From the pull-down menu, use "Open" to select the image to be cropped.

- Select the crop tool (rectangle) from the toolbar on the left vertical toolbar.
- Click and hold using the crosshair to define a region to be cropped.
- Let go of the button to select the region.
- Click and hold within the box to reposition.
- From under "Edit" pull-down menu, select "Copy" to place the image on a clipboard.
- Under the "File" pull-down menu, select "New" and then "Image From Clipboard."

Adjusting the Size of an Image

When cropping or importing an image from another source, it is possible that the size of the image may not be appropriate for the intended use in the e-portfolio. Whenever an image is imported into the PowerPoint program as a JPEG image, it is usually possible to click on the image and find the "handles," which appear as squares on each corner and in the middle of each line. By clicking on the handles, it is possible to stretch the image with the handles on the sides or size the image by clicking on the corner handles and then dragging to extend or reduce both dimensions that define the corner. However, if the image is to remain an external file so as to limit the size of the PowerPoint presentation file, then the size at which the image will display is not as easily adjusted. As will be discussed in Chapter 9, the size of the image may be too large or too small as a result of how the image was digitally created. This applies to an image that was cut from another image in the "cropping" procedure described earlier. PhotoShop Elements will allow the adjustment of this image size, which can then be saved as a new image in a new size. Use the following steps to size the image:

- Open PhotoShop Elements.
- Open the image to be resized.
- Choose "Resize" from the "Image" pull-down menu.
- Select "Image Size" from the pop-up menu.
- Choose the size most appropriate (usually 72–96 dpi).
- Use "Save As" to save the image with a different name.

The technical meaning of these measurements is found in Chapter 9, but let it suffice at this point that the selection of these sizes most nearly matches the capability of a computer screen to display the image. Saving the image as a different name will allow the image to be saved and then hyperlinked to an e-portfolio as an appropriately sized image. This capacity of PhotoShop Elements will make the e-portfolio more viewer-friendly by preparing the images for easy viewing.

Masking Part of an Image: Filtering

When importing images into an e-portfolio file, the author may notice that the image shows an unintended feature. The feature may be a location name, address, or even a person. Even if you have permission to use the photograph, the imperative to protect anonymity is paramount. Any clues to the identity of the individuals should be protected to the greatest extent possible. If, for example, an evaluation is used as an e-portfolio artifact and that evaluation is in a Word file, the name of the author should be deleted. A handwritten file, however, represents a special challenge because the signature, as a graphic, may not be easily deleted without making the document appear quite suspicious. In PhotoShop Elements, a tool allows you to mask the sensitive information by using a range of special effects. These range from completely blackening a region of the image to blurring part of the image by making it appear as if you are looking through patterned "bathroom window" glass. By blurring the name of the company on an image of a plant in which a manager experienced success, masking a signature on a handwritten note of appreciation, or blurring a face accidentally captured in a photograph, the e-portfolio author is meeting the promise of protecting identities.

Refer to the Student Resource CD for 2007 Microsoft and Mac screenshots

PhotoShop Elements makes filtering quite easy. Screenshot 8.2 shows an image with a region outlined by the lasso tool and the selection for distorting using the glass appearance. This results in a distortion similar to that when looking through "security glass" (see Screenshot 8.3).

Follow the steps below to filter parts of an image:

- Open PhotoShop Elements.
- Open the image that includes a region to be filtered.
- Choose the "Lasso" to select an irregular shape or the rectangle to select a regular shape.
- Outline the region to be filtered with the tool chosen.
- Choose the "Filter" pull-down menu, and select the filter type from the window.
- Apply the filter by clicking on the selected filter type.

Filters range from effects that will blur parts of an image to transparent patterns that will create the appearance that the image has been painted with brushstrokes. Saving the image will also save the effect of the filter.

Adjusting for Brightness (Color, Contrast, and Brightness)

Poor quality of color, lack of contrast, and too much or too little brightness are some of the problems that could face an author as digital images are prepared for e-portfolio use. In film photography, such characteristics of images are difficult for a novice to correct, but the digital dimension allows the portfolio author to adjust these character-istics more easily. An image that is taken indoors and too far away from the intended subject may result in an image too dark for use. A flash image taken too close to the subject may be overexposed, washing out color and detail from the subject. The lighting of a subject may cause the subject to appear the wrong color. This effect can be caused, for example, by sodium vapor lights that make a person appear more green than normal. Follow the steps below to correct any of these problems in digital images:

- Open PhotoShop Elements.
- Open the image that needs adjustment.
- Select "Enhance" from the pull-down menu.
- Choose automatic adjustment of contrast, color, or red-eye.
- Continue to the next step if Auto Levels does not correct the problem.
- Select "Enhance" from the pull-down menu.
- Select "Adjust Color" or "Adjust Smart Fix" as required.
- Use the sliding tools to apply changes.
- Saving the image will save the new settings.

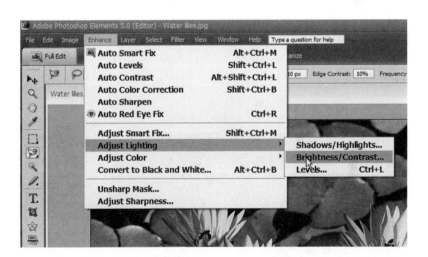

❖ EDITING SOUND

Programs do exist for editing sound files. In most situations, they can be easily located and downloaded as "shareware" from the World

Wide Web. Examples might include VideoStudio 7 (www.ulead.com/us/runme.htm), Goldwave (www.goldwave.com), or Electronic Musician (emusician.com/audio_editing_software). These programs permit a sound file to be played while the editing program tracks the sound on a display that looks something like a seismogram. Concurrently, a timer is active and displays on the screen.

The user can select a sound clip by either time alone or by looking at the sound display and cutting at an appropriate point in the music. Sound editing software also allows for cutting segments out of music.

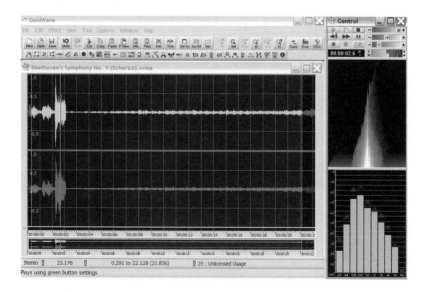

It is possible that a section of a song to be used in an e-portfolio has a stanza with questionable wording. Perhaps the use of expletives or images of violence or sexual content make the stanza undesirable. In that case, using a combination of timing and watching the display, a single stanza or any section of any length can be cut out of a sound file.

It is important to remember that PowerPoint can accept music clips in several of the most common formats, including ".wav" and ".mp3." It is important to recall, however, that there are limits to the legal use of audio clips that may be produced for commercial use. However, with the permission granted by the TEACH Act, it is possible to import music into these editing programs from CDs and then save it in a PowerPoint-friendly format. Most common sound-editing software packages are available as free downloads from the Web. The use of any of these software packages requires practice to generate the desired output. The differences among the packages are so great that including details other than those above would be counterproductive for this writing effort. The best way to become proficient in editing sound is to simply find a program and use it.

❖ EDITING VIDEO

Video editing has been a function reserved for large movie studios, where the art of cutting and splicing film is a highly valued skill. Although video editing still remains a technical skill that is an art, the technology of cutting and splicing is no longer reserved for the large studios. Film requires physical cuts and physical pasting, but digital video requires much simplified virtual cutting and virtual pasting. The programs to accomplish video editing have also become more common with programs such as iMovie for the Macintosh, Adobe Premiere for Windows-based computers, or Windows Movie Maker. With any video-editing program, you need to experiment with the program to become proficient. Importing video clips and editing are done in real time but often at the cost of a most valuable resource—time. Again, the programs that are available are numerous, and going into any level of detail would be beyond the scope of this work. However, some characteristics can be reviewed here.

Importing video requires the real-time playback of video. A USB connection may be sufficient for the review of digital photography, but digital video represents much more data than pictures one at a time.

USB technology is not sufficient for video work. Most new video cameras have a feature that allows for the wide bandwidth (i.e., very fast) digital import of video through "IEEE 1394" data exchange technology (also called "iLink" in Sony terminology and the more common "firewire" in Apple terminology). Connecting the camera to an "IEEE 1394" port on your computer or connecting the camera to play back through a digitizer is necessary to import video saved on tape. The function of a digitizer is to convert the standard video signal to a digital format that can be recognized by a computer. To make a movie, you must save a digital video clip or a series of clips and export it as a "movie." The steps to accomplish this are generally as follows:

- Connect the camera to the computer through a digitizer or firewire port.
- Start the video-editing software.
- Begin to play the video through the camera.
- Click on "Import Video" to start capturing a clip in the video-editing software.
- Click on "Import Video" again to stop the capture of a particular clip.
- Repeat using "Import Video" as a toggle to capture clips.
- Drag selected clips to the "video" or "movie bar" in the editing window.
- Drag clips to rearrange them in the order desired.
- Add special video effects as required and permitted by the software.
- Add voiceover or music as required and permitted by the software.
- "Export" the product as a movie, specifying the file as a .mov format.

Video editing allows the user to select segments from digital video to include in a final product. It is recommended that if video is to be cut into small segments, the video should be cut upon its initial capture for inclusion in the edited product or movie. The reason for this is that the clips can be included in the movie, their locations or order can subsequently be changed, or the clips can be deleted. These operations, however, are accomplished clip by clip. Thus, if there is a possibility that one answer in an interview will need to be deleted from a movie being made for an e-portfolio, then the interview should be saved as a series of video clips. This will allow appropriate video clips to be made as part of the movie, and the inappropriate clips can be deleted.

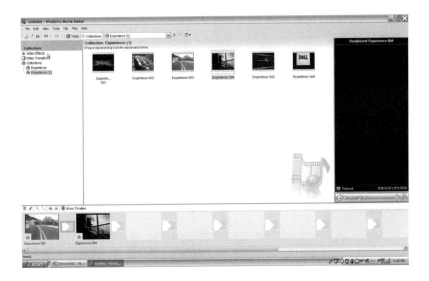

The display that is part of video editing is very similar to the display used for sound editing. A timer is shown, as is a pair of graphic displays of both audio and video segments included in the movie. Segments that make up the movie can be cut, moved, and deleted individually. It is possible to remove the video from one segment by using the video display while keeping the audio intact. It is possible to delete the audio from a video segment and then unite the video with the audio from another source. A variety of video effects is also standard with video-editing programs. You can fade to black at the end of one segment and then introduce the next segment by fade in from black. This would be an example of how only studios could do video editing. It is why studios were once the only source of technology able to produce a video where you would continue hearing an interview while cutting the video to a listener who is reacting to the video. Such manipulations of video are possible with the editing software that is available.

It bears repeating here that only enough audio or video should be included in an e-portfolio as necessary to make a point. Too much audio and video can be a distraction from the e-portfolio. Thus, it is recommended that these files be saved outside of the PowerPoint e-portfolio and that hyperlinks be established to allow the viewer to go to those clips only if they find a need to do so. In addition, the audio and video that might be included in an e-portfolio ought to be of high quality. Poor artifact files, or even poor audio or video, can work against a positive evaluation of the e-portfolio as an assessment tool. The purpose of the e-portfolio is defined by the e-portfolio's ability to

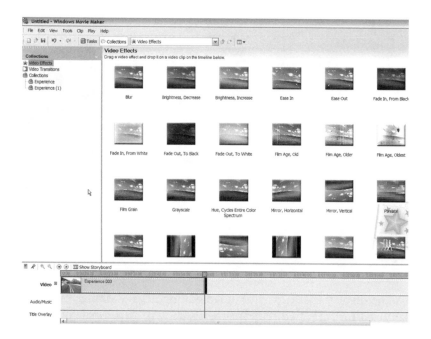

demonstrate that it meets the specified requirements or standards. In addition, audio and video files are relatively large in terms of the demand for memory. A 15-minute teaching segment, for example, will yield a digital video clip of about 1 gigabyte in size. Thus, to accommodate viewers who may not have systems with a large memory, you should not include audio or video directly in the PowerPoint presentation file that is to become an e-portfolio.

SUMMARY

In this chapter, the value of hyperlinking the e-portfolio is featured as the element that elevates the e-portfolio above that of its print equivalent. Hyperlinking between and among slides is augmented by hyperlinking to and among artifact files. It is hyperlinking that permits the e-portfolio author to exercise creativity to make the PowerPoint presentation a nonlinear experience. This permits a viewer to move directly to standards and artifacts of interest.

The chapter also addressed issues of artifact quality. Images can be edited using the Adobe PhotoShop Elements program. Although its capabilities are far beyond those outlined in the chapter, the program can easily address the four common problems discussed in the text. Audio and video editing can be accomplished with widely available "shareware" downloaded from the Internet or software prepackaged with some computers. A general discussion of this process is presented, and users are encouraged to explore the specific requirements of the downloaded program by practicing with it. Although editing images, audio, and video is a skill, the programs now available make these operations possible, with an appropriate investment of time, for the novice e-portfolio author.

QUESTIONS TO GUIDE E-PORTFOLIO PREPARATION

1. Describe how a school superintendent, conducting interviews for a master classroom manager, might appreciate using a nonlinear e-portfolio rather than a linear portfolio.

2. What is the difference between internal and external hyperlinking in a nonlinear e-portfolio?

3. What are four very basic functions that can be accomplished through the use of Adobe's PhotoShop Elements editing application?

4. Name two applications that can be used to edit sound, and identify which of the options you identify are available to you in your computer lab or on your computer.

5. Name two video-editing applications and identify which of the options you identify are available to you in your computer lab or on your computer.

6. List four circumstances that may appear in digital photos or video that would require the use of editing applications.

9

Tools You Can Use

Focus Questions

- What are common tools an e-portfolio author might use?
- How can images and video be captured for inclusion in e-portfolios?
- What portable media can be used to save e-portfolios?
- What formats of CDs and DVDs are available on which e-portfolios can be saved?

❖ INTRODUCTION

The construction of an e-portfolio as presented in this book demands the use of a variety of tools that are all intended to create files to serve as artifacts within the e-portfolio. These tools include but are not limited to scanners, digital cameras, digital video cameras, digitizers, and memory devices such as CD and DVD burners. The purpose of this chapter is to examine some of the tools that are on the market and available for use in e-portfolio development. The coverage of any of the items listed above is purposefully brief, for there is no way within the pages of a single book to cover the entire spectrum of the models or the bells and whistles that are available. The chapter instead will outline some of those features that all of the tools have in common, and the descriptions will offer a bit more specificity on those features that are widely available. The users' guide of the specific model of any tool that you have available will clarify what features, functions, and limitations might exist with the equipment and software you have available for use in your particular situation. The chapter will consider the tools in broad categories of still images, digital video, and sound. Specialized programs that will allow the customization of those features will be addressed within each section.

❖ COLLECTING DOCUMENTS FOR THE PORTFOLIO

Documents are easiest to collect, for virtually any document can be saved in a format that can be accessed by PowerPoint. We recommend that all documents be in MS Word. If a document is not in MS Word, there are several ways to move it into that format. Word-processing programs all have a window when the option "Save As" is selected from the file pull-down menu. The ability to change the format of the document is in a window that will read, in some way, "Save As File Type." The window will be set in default to the file type created by the program being used. Typically, an arrow allows the author to select from a series of options. Select the Microsoft Word, MS Word, or Word option that proves to be effective when selected. The only way to know for sure is to save the file in this revised type and test it with MS Word.

If there is no success in saving the file in an MS Word format, it is usually possible to save the file as a "rich text file" or RTF. A text file reduces the contents to the basic language of the computer but loses most of the formatting (spacing, indentations, underlining, italics, and even font type). An RTF file is a text file but is an option that has been made "rich" because it will keep more of the formatting than a simple text file. To import the RTF file into MS Word, follow the steps below:

- Start MS Word.
- Select "Open" under the "File" pull-down menu.
- Adjust the window to allow all readable files.
- Select the RTF files of interest.
- Select "Open."

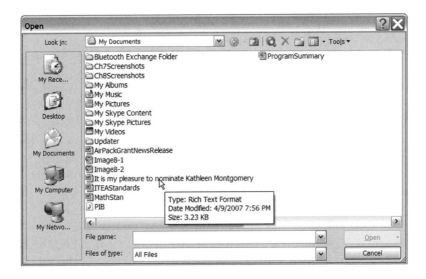

- Edit as necessary.
- Select "Save As" under the "File" pull-down menu.
- Adjust file type to identify the file as an MS Word document.
- Save as a new file (add extension if needed).

You may have to do some editing to account for the lost formatting, but that will prove, in most cases, less time-consuming than creating the file from scratch.

Additional information is in order for Macintosh users. Macintosh computers will read files saved on IBM-formatted disks. Thus, taking a file from an IBM-formatted disk is not a problem if you still use disks. However, if a file is being imported into a Macintosh environment for the construction of an e-portfolio, the e-portfolio may be accessed in the Windows environment. Thus, if you are saving a file for use in the e-portfolio, it may be necessary for you to add the extension ".doc" to the filename. In the Windows environment, the MS Word program will expect that extension. If the hyperlink to a document does not have the extension, the e-portfolio may not work when run in the Windows environment. Regardless of environment, a "flash drive" can be read by any computer with USB capability. If the computer is somewhat dated, a driver may have to be downloaded, but all computers running Windows XT or Mac OSX will have the drivers for flash drives already installed. A caution is noted here for the record and not from experience: Flash memory degrades over time. Thus, if your presentation, documents, and other files are important, back them up on optical disks (CD or DVD) or on a hard drive.

It is possible for a scanner to capture a print document and save it in a word-processing format that can be imported into the MS Word program. In our experience, though, a great deal of editing is required to recover the document as a high-quality word-processing document. In many cases, it becomes easier to reenter the document or save the document as a JPEG graphics image rather than try to scan it into a new document. To capture a document with a scanner, you need to select the appropriate settings on the scanner. Once the scanner creates the graphics file, the file is imported into MS Word by selecting "File" and "Open" and then using the pop-up window that opens. The pop-up window will allow the author to browse files (in the Windows environment) or select a file (in the Macintosh environment) to find the file as it was saved after scanning. When the "Open" button is clicked, MS Word will open and convert the file. The author then saves the file containing the document image as any other MS Word document. We encourage, for instance, our teacher candidates to include classroom observations with lesson plans to increase the value of the lesson plan as an artifact. This is done by adding pages (as required) to the end of the lesson plan, scanning supervisor observations, and then inserting the scan (as a JPEG graphics file) onto the blank pages following the lesson plan.

❖   OF DOTS AND PIXELS: IMAGE SIZES

Before proceeding, it is necessary to understand how images are saved as digital files and how monitors display those images. This is a prerequisite for understanding the settings that might be needed on digital cameras and scanners. An image as displayed on a computer depends on the apparent blending of colors represented by tiny color blotches called pixels. Each pixel displays a single color determined by a combination of how bright three different display colors glow. These colors, built into each pixel, are red, green, and blue. This is the origin of the term *RGB*, which some people use to describe color computer monitors. Most monitors have a finite number of pixels available. The higher the quality of the monitor, the more dense the number of pixels available. Most 15-inch monitors on the market are 1024 pixels across by 768 pixels high (1024 × 768 pixels). Monitors that are 17 inches are also commonly about

1024×768 pixels. A high-density 17-inch monitor may have 1280×1024 pixels or more. The Apple Cinema monitor, a wide-screen monitor that has a targeted use, is 1680×1050 pixels. The number of pixels available on a monitor is important to recall when scanning color images or taking color photographs. The number represents a real limit to how the images are displayed on a computer monitor.

A photograph or a scan is accomplished by breaking the image into tiny sections called dots. The scanner or camera establishes what single (average) color settings are appropriate for each section when the image is displayed. The digital code for the color settings of each dot is what is saved as the digital image. The smaller and more dense the dot, the clearer the image will be as the higher numbers of smaller, distinct colors blend more smoothly into one another. However, the smaller the dot, the more dots it will take to completely digitize the image. This dot density is usually indicated by the term *dots per inch* (dpi). The more dpi, the more memory the scan or picture will require. Images are usually of sufficient quality for e-portfolios if the image is 640×480 dpi.

When the photographed or scanned image is viewed on a computer, the computer will interpret each dot as the setting for a pixel. Thus, 640×480 dpi is the appropriate size given the number of pixels on most computer monitors. As you increase the number of dots that comprise the image, a corresponding number of pixels will be required to display the image. Thus, the quality of an image that is 640×480 dpi will degrade if the image is "blown up" to a larger size, for each dot will increase in size as the image is expanded. If enlarged sufficiently, the dots will not display an image that is very smooth. The borders, for example, between the relatively light skintone of a person will not grade smoothly into the darker tones of the cheek. Instead, you may actually see the squares of color as the dots increase in size to the point they can be sensed when viewing the image.

When an image with a larger number of dots is displayed, the image size will become bigger as more pixels are required to view the image. The number of dots per inch can be so high that the computer has insufficient numbers of pixels to display each dot, and the image can exceed the limits of the monitor, extending beyond its edges. Sizing the image may be required. This very large size would be excellent, however, if the objective were to produce a very large image. The high number of dots would mean that the image would continue to be smooth when the large image is viewed. Is this quality necessary for most applications of the e-portfolio? Absolutely not.

❖ SCANNING MATERIALS FOR USE AS ARTIFACTS

The scanner is either a freestanding or peripheral device (attached to a computer) used to create digital files of print materials. The scanner can create digital files that can be imported as word-processing documents or as graphic images. The number of types of scanners is as many as there are types of computers, yet they fall into two basic categories. The flatbed scanner has a large glass plate on which the document is laid before scanning. In this type of scanner, the document remains still while the imaging hardware inside the scanner moves to capture the entire document. The operation of this type of scanner is like most of the plain paper copiers on the market today. In fact, plain paper copiers are now using the scanner technology to make the copies that are produced. The other type of scanner is the sheet-fed scanner. Its operation is like most fax machines in that the document is fed into the scanner, one sheet at a time. As the sheet goes through the scanner, the scanning hardware in the machine remains motionless while the sheet passes through. These scanners tend to be smaller but often take more time than many flatbed scanners. Like the computer technology they are built for, scanners have developed quickly and are now much less difficult to operate than when they first made their appearance in the technology market.

The operation of a freestanding scanner is a matter of selecting the appropriate settings either on the face of the scanner or in the scanning software running on the computer. Once this is done, you can then initiate the scan. The scan is usually saved to a documents file or, in the case of freestanding scanners, to portable media devices. The typical settings include "Scan Color," "Compression," "Resolution," and "Scan Area." "Scan Color" allows the user to establish whether the scan should be in color, gray tones, or black and white. Although black and white requires less memory, this should be selected when you need to scan a word-processing document. When scanning a picture, use at least shades of gray tones, but color is best for photographs in color. Compression refers to how the scan is saved. A scan saved as high compression will take a little longer but will occupy half the memory as a scan saved with low compression. The scan area determines how much of the space available will be used on a flatbed or how long the scan equipment in a sheet-fed scanner will remain active. If an 8½ × 11-inch printed document is being scanned, select "Letter Size." If a 3 × 4-inch picture is being scanned, select "Auto" to limit the area being saved to the scan. For most applications of the e-portfolio, a low resolution (a smaller dpi scan, as explained earlier) is appropriate to save memory yet produce an image sufficient for most e-portfolios. Follow the steps below to capture an image appropriate for inclusion in an e-portfolio:

- Turn on the scanner.
- Place the image source (picture, etc.) on the glass.
- Ensure that the location of the image source is correct.
- Cover the image with the scanner's cover.
- Check that the destination is set to receive the saved file.
- Set scan mode to color.
- Set image quality to 300 dpi.
- Give the image a filename for which it will be known.
- Establish what type of file it will be saved as.
- Provide the destination for saving the file.
- Press the button to start the scan.

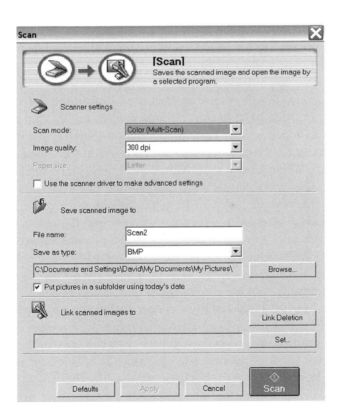

The operation of a peripheral scanner is largely dependent on the software that is loaded into the computer. Generally, the software is loaded into the computer to make scanning dependent only on navigation through the menus of the software. This will include the options as described above in the operation of a freestanding scanner. However, a computer peripheral will have one additional requirement not present on a freestanding scanner—a location for the file to be saved must be identified. A freestanding scanner will automatically save the file to the disk or other portable media that is inserted into the scanner. A peripheral will ask, in a window, where the file should be saved. Other than this difference, the basic operation of any peripheral scanner, regardless of whether the scanner is a flatbed or sheet-fed scanner, is similar to the freestanding scanner. The PowerPoint program is limited in that a graphics image should be scanned such that the image is saved in JPEG, a format easily recognized by the program.

❖ USING DIGITAL CAMERAS TO CAPTURE IMAGES

Digital cameras are becoming more common than cameras that use film. In a recent visit to an electronics store, we noted that there were precious few optical film cameras compared to the larger variety of digital cameras. Furthermore, most of the companies that have traditionally produced most of the common consumer film cameras have begun to produce equally high-quality digital cameras. The quality of digital cameras is largely dependent on the size of the image (dots per inch) that the camera will save. Although "1-megapixel" memories are available, they are woefully short on quality of the image. It is recommended that a digital camera have the potential for a minimum of 3-megapixel images, with 5-megapixel cameras being at the high end of need for most e-portfolio uses. An 8-megapixel capability camera, with optional manual controls, large optical zoom, and single lens reflex (aim through the same lens as the image is placed into memory), produces images that are equivalent to quality professional film cameras. Of course, high-quality cameras only produce high-quality images if the instrument is handled by a professional.

The terminology here is important—a film camera that has features such as automatic focus may use electronic technology for its operation, but it is not necessarily a digital camera. The digital camera saves images as digital files that are necessary formats to be transferred into an e-portfolio. Yet another option exists for the consumer. Some traditional film developers offer to have your film developed and also saved in digital formats and returned as CDs. The CDs generally arrive packaged with software that can be used to covert the images to the JPEG format, which can be inserted into e-portfolios.

Another feature that may be available for the digital camera is a zoom feature that the digital camera accomplishes in one of two different ways. The optical zoom uses the optical lens to decrease the apparent distance to an object. This has the advantage of maintaining the dpi of the image, for even though the apparent distance is reduced, the number of dpi in the image remains the same. Zooming in this manner is superior to the digital zoom. The digital zoom expands the image by limiting the size of the image and expanding it to fill the display. This reduces the number of dots and degrades the quality of the image. This may be noticeable only if the image is enlarged or viewed on a large display, but it does represent a problem if there is a need to further crop or alter a photograph. Thus, a 3-megapixel camera with an optical zoom is the minimum recommendation.

The operation of the digital camera is not unlike the operation of an electronic film camera. The difference between the digital camera and the film camera is how the camera saves the image and how it is downloaded into a computer program. Digital cameras are usually equipped with an onboard memory, but it is very limited. Thus, digital cameras usually save to digital media. Some cameras save to floppy disks or mini disks. These require an appropriate disk drive to download the image into files on a computer. Other digital cameras use a "memory stick" or "memory card" to save images on RAM, which is built into the card. These cameras will download images, depending on the camera model and capabilities, by using a cable (usually USB cables) or by accessing "card readers," a peripheral attached or built into the computer for the specific purpose of reading digital camera memory cards. The specific requirements of the camera you choose will be an important part of the operation manual that you will need to read carefully. The downloading of pictures can be as easy as accessing the camera as if it were an additional USB peripheral to your computer or accessing a memory card the same way that we access a USB flash drive.

❖ A FEW PHOTOGRAPHY HINTS

A hint or two for digital photography is warranted here. Options of autofocus can make the camera as easy as the easiest "point-and-shoot" film camera. The camera is aimed at the image, the shutter is partially depressed, a beep is heard as the camera completes its focus, and the shutter is depressed the rest of the way. In practice, however, there may be a slight delay between the click of the shutter and the capture of the image. A digital photographer thinks slightly "in front" of the time at which the subject is imaged to obtain the image desired. There is a need, in some situations, to anticipate the shot that you are trying to capture and click the "shutter" appropriately. The images that are captured should be of a high quality. Low-quality images such as those with subjects out of focus or poorly staged images can work against the production of a high-quality e-portfolio. Options to use programs for editing digital images are presented in Chapter 8. The common program for this purpose is PhotoShop Elements. The PhotoShop Elements application can be used to adjust color or light, crop, and/or size photographs as required. Adobe PhotoShop Elements can be used for photographic effects that are actually quite advanced, yet it is relatively easy to master those elementary adjustments to photographic images that may improve those images for your e-portfolios.

Try to avoid images that look like police mug shots (do not square the subject to the camera lens). For portraits, have individuals stand or sit at an acute angle to the camera and look at the lens. The portrait should capture the upper body but not much above the top of the head. Informal images should be either well framed or action shots. Framing uses materials in the foreground or background to focus attention on the object being shot. The good tropical sunset shot, for instance, has a palm tree in the foreground positioned on the left side of the image with its fronds across the top of the image. The subject, the sunset in this example, is framed by the structure of the palm tree. Another example would have a person imaged standing nearly sideways to point to a poster and speak to an audience about a project rather than having a person posed standing in front of the poster, all square to the camera. The poster and the setting of the presentation will frame the subject—the presenter in this example. These pointers will also help to ensure that the subject appears naturally doing what you may be trying to capture. Even the portrait, or "head shot," used to provide a more formal picture of a person follows these rules. The best head shots show the subject when the shoulders are not squared, and a background is used that is not intrusive yet serves to frame the subject. Using some of these hints, the mug shot can be reserved for its traditional role in police files.

One final comment is needed, and it is posed in terms of a question: How do you believe a picture of yourself will affect the assessment of your e-portfolio? It must be remembered that federal law prohibits discrimination on the basis of many factors that will be exposed if e-portfolio authors choose to include digital images of themselves. Is it possible that the inclusion of the intentional or unintentional image of yourself may influence the assessor, consciously or subconsciously? Would the image be better left out than placed in the presentation? There is some truth in the old maxim that beauty, after all, is in the eye of the beholder. Perhaps this is a question that all e-portfolio authors must consider on their own to make an informed decision based, in part, on the purpose of the e-portfolio. There is no single definitive answer. We suggest, though, that unless there is a clear reason to do so, you should avoid including your own image.

❖ CAPTURING AND USING DIGITAL VIDEO

Digital video can be captured with a variety of technologies. Most digital cameras (discussed earlier) have options for capturing short video sequences (on the order of 5 seconds). This video is downloaded as with still images, depending on the camera design. The short video is saved to the internal memory, disk media, or memory card and downloaded along with the still images that are part of the memory in whatever form it takes. In many cases, the video needs to be converted to a format that is useable by the PowerPoint program. It is a strength of the program that PowerPoint does convert most of the video formats automatically for inclusion into the PowerPoint program. For longer video sequences, the use of either digital video cameras or digitizing equipment will be necessary. A general format for developing a video clip "movie" for an e-portfolio is presented in Chapter 8.

Digital video cameras, like their still counterparts, are down in price to the point that they are affordable when there is a need for them. The operation of these video cameras is very similar to a standard video camera in that they are usually equipped with zoom, start/stop record buttons, and a number of special effects onboard. Depending on the specific video camera model that is purchased, the image can be saved to tape or to other types of media such as memory cards or memory sticks. Short video obtained through digital cameras can be downloaded using the USB technology and programs standard with the camera. Longer video, such as that imported through digital video cameras, usually requires "IEEE 1394" (or "firewire") capability, mostly with the assistance of a program that is standard with the hardware. The program that accepts longer video segments will also allow for the editing of the video with options, including the selection and deletion of segments that are and are not desired. The video that is downloaded is usually in a format indicated as .mov, a format that is supported by PowerPoint. Even when the video clip is not automatically in .mov or is a shorter MPEG video clip, the video-editing programs can convert the file easily to PowerPoint-friendly formats.

A digitizer is another way to capture video for inclusion in a presentation. Digitizers can be purchased for a number of purposes, including digitizing standard videotape and movie film. A digitizer is a computer peripheral that accepts a nondigital input and converts the signal to a digital format. The most commonly used digitizers have standard video saved on videocassettes. Using a program such as iMovie or Adobe Premiere, a video sequence from a videocassette can be captured and edited for what is needed for the e-portfolio.

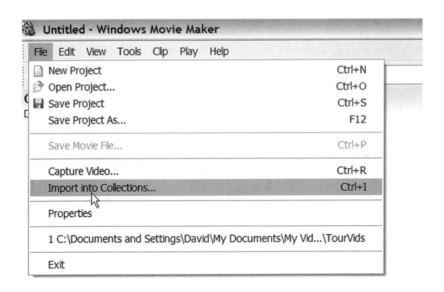

Desired sections, called clips, can be retained, and that which is not desired can be deleted from the sequence. Once the sequence is edited as might be desired, the sequence can be saved as a file that can be accessed by PowerPoint.

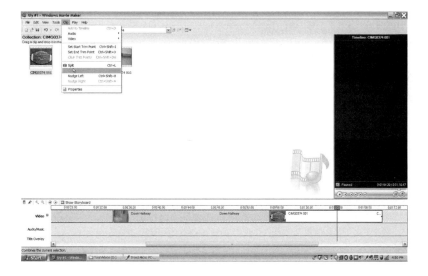

The software that can be used to edit these video clips is discussed in Chapter 8.

The use of audio or video in an e-portfolio should be limited to only those segments necessary to validate how authors argue that they meet the requirements or standards as set forward in their reflections. To include audio and/or video in an e-portfolio, especially one that is lengthy, purely for the purpose of showing that it can be done is a possible detractor from the purpose of the e-portfolio. Additional considerations, discussed in Chapter 8, include issues of the quality of the audio and the video as well as the memory required for audio and video files. It must be remembered that an e-portfolio is being prepared for a purpose, and materials ought to be included only if they forward the purpose of the e-portfolio. Hyperlinks to poor-quality video or to audio files that may be favorites but not directly involved in a requirement or standard may speak against the learning that an e-portfolio attempts to communicate.

❖ SAVING A PORTFOLIO TO MEDIA

Saving an e-portfolio can represent a difficult decision. In the past, most computer users were comfortable with saving files on a hard drive or to 3.5-inch disks. They are, however, outdated. A floppy disk (3.5-inch disk) will hold a fixed amount of material. The IBM-formatted double high-density (2HD) disk will hold about 1.44 megabytes of information, while the 2HD disk for the Macintosh will hold about 1.40 megabytes. This may be sufficient for small e-portfolios in the amount of information they contain. However, images are very common in e-portfolio construction, with each image occupying a large amount of space. One small graphic image may still demand more than 50K of memory. A high-quality image may occupy more than 800K. As the images become more complex, the available space on a floppy disk (1.4 megabytes is equivalent to 1,400K) will begin to approach the limit. Even more demanding in terms of disk space are motion and music. It is very easy to approach the limit of 700 megs of a CD-R given the increasing creativity of e-portfolio authors and the hardware that makes it possible to easily save virtually any evidence in a digital format.

Floppy disks (3.5-inch disks) are not sufficient to save an e-portfolio, and given the obvious limitations of distributing files saved on a hard drive, optical storage devices have become standard on many computer systems. Both CD- and DVD-recording software and hardware make it possible to save 650 megabytes, and a DVD has a possible capacity of 4.7 gigabytes (equivalent to 4,700 megabytes). The high capacity of these optical data storage media makes it possible to easily save any e-portfolio. A DVD, for example, will hold up to 120 minutes of video! It is the rare candidate who would approach this in an e-portfolio, even with the inclusion of one or more snippets to serve as artifacts. Because there are many manufacturers of CD and DVD equipment, providing specific instructions for saving materials on CD and DVD is not practical. Some instruction, however, will provide direction that is consistent from system to system. The remainder of this chapter will briefly consider the process involved in creating a CD or DVD.

❖ BURNING A CD

Many things are necessary to understand before creating a CD-ROM of an e-portfolio. When material is saved to a CD, the process is called "burning" because a small laser actually "engraves" the information onto tracks that surround the center of the CD. The shape (size and depth) of the engraving is how the CD reader optically recovers the information. For those with sufficient life experience, this can be compared to a very highly improved "LP record." The CD, however, is read by a laser rather than by the physical contact of a needle. As the differences made by the laser are quite small, it is important to protect the CD from scratches or smudges that would interfere with the optical reading of the saved data. Most of us are familiar with the "skipping" that can happen with music CDs that are scratched. The same thing can happen when one attempts to access data if the CD is scratched. Proper protection and care should be taken when transporting and handling data CDs.

It is first important to recognize that data can be saved to two CD types. The CD-R media are one-time use media. It is therefore important to have everything that is to be on the CD ready to be saved at the same time. Once a CD-R has been used to save data, accessing, reusing, or recovering unused space will be impossible. Preparing for burning an e-portfolio onto a CD-R, therefore, must be done carefully. If files are in multiple locations, for example, these files must be incorporated such that they can all be accessed for the burn. A folder must be created to host all of the files, both the PowerPoint e-portfolio file as well as all artifact files imported from a host of sources, whether they are from flash drives, card readers from cameras, or e-mail attachments. That folder is then burned to the CD-R along with a "Read Me First" MS Word file that we recommend writing. If the artifact files are saved first, then it would not be possible to add the PowerPoint e-portfolio since CD-R is a one-time burn technology. This limitation is why we cannot underscore the importance of burning a folder containing all of the artifact files and the PowerPoint portfolio, as well as a separate "Read Me First" file.

The CD-RW is a CD type on which changes can be made, materials added, and presentations altered. CD-RW disks use a format, however, that may not be equally accessible from all computers. In other words, a CD-RW made with one type of computer with one type of CD-RW burner may need that same computer type and/or same CD burner to read the data from the CD itself. The utility of CD-RW technology is severely limited to specific hardware capabilities and is thus not recommended for making e-portfolio copies for distribution. This type of CD may be used by the e-portfolio author for updating and saving the files and the presentation. Using the same computer and CD-burning hardware will make it possible to alter files as new and improved artifacts become available, and the PowerPoint e-portfolio can be similarly updated and tested. However, when it is time to distribute the CD, it is highly recommended that the CD-R be used rather than the CD-RW. It is important to remember that the entire set of files on a CD-RW is saved when even only one file is updated. This presents the possibility of presenting the author with memory problems. In this event, burning to a new disk is the answer to the problem.

The specific instructions for burning a CD should be provided by the makers of the specific hardware and software that you are using. However, most software provides a "click-and-drag" feature to move files into an area identified to list files that are to be burned. When using CD-Rs, if all files, including the PowerPoint e-portfolio, are located in the same folder, only one folder will be moved to this area. For the operation of PowerPoint, it is critical that the location of all files referenced by a hyperlink be referenced for their location following the burning. Referencing hyperlinked artifacts is easiest when both the artifacts and PowerPoint are found within the same folder. In fact, relative hyperlinking is assumed by the current versions of MS PowerPoint only if the presentation and the artifacts are in the same folder. Thus, if the artifacts are saved in a single folder and PowerPoint is saved separately, the hyperlinks will not work on any computer except that single computer on which the presentation was authored. While earlier versions of PowerPoint would allow for the designation of a "relative hyperlink" on the hyperlinking pop-up menu, this option is no longer present. Rather, PowerPoint will look for relatively hyperlinked files only within the same folder as the presentation is found.

Several formats exist for data to be saved to CDs. A format exists to save information on CDs specifically for the Windows environment, another specifically for the Macintosh environment, and yet another that will read across platforms. ISO refers to the International Organization for Standardization, which has established standards for data storage. ISO Level 1 and Level 2 are specifically designed for the Windows environment. These formats require the dot and three-letter extension to all filenames to be saved. Examples are .doc, .xls, and .jpg for MS Word documents, Excel spreadsheets, and JPEG images, respectively. Although Level 1 limits filenames to 8 characters (plus the extension), Level 2 will allow filenames of 32 characters. Filenames in these formats should also avoid characters such as a dash, comma, and space. A data format called ISO 9660 (called Apple Extended format in the Macintosh environment) creates one set of data that is Windows-friendly and a separate version that is Macintosh-friendly. A format known as Joliet is capable of saving information in a DOS-friendly format as well as the Windows format. Because an e-portfolio author is never really sure of the platform that a viewer might be using, the ISO 9660 format is the preferred choice. In fact, most computers will use this format as the default for all CD-R burning. Thus, in virtually every case, Macintosh- or Windows-based machines both will run the default CD-R-burned e-portfolio PowerPoint presentation.

PowerPoint 2007 Note:

Please recall that Office 2007 saves files in a completely different format than Office 2003. The files are backward compatible. That is, PowerPoint 2007 can open a presentation and related files composed in PowerPoint 2003. However, the files are not forward compatible. That is, a presentation written using PowerPoint 2007 will not open using PowerPoint 2003. Thus, it is important to save presentations written in PowerPoint 2007 "as file type" PowerPoint 1998-2003 to allow an older machine to read the file.

Once the format is selected, there may be a prompt to establish how data are to be stored. Disk-at-once (DAO) recording will be the most common means of creating the CD. It will record all sections and the entire CD at the same time. CDs have introductory information as well as information to close out the CD. The DAO setting will record, as the name implies, all at once. Some projects need to be written one "piece" at a time. A CD-R writer that allows TAO is capable of allowing the recorded material to remain unfinished. Additional information is then added as a separate "track," with up to 99 tracks possible on a single CD. Additional information is recorded to the CD to link the tracks together before the CD is completed. The easiest and most direct way of producing an e-portfolio is DAO recording. Follow the steps below to burn a CD:

- Create a folder in "My Documents" or on the hard drive.
- Place all artifact files and the PowerPoint portfolio in the folder.
- Check to ensure that the PowerPoint portfolio presentation runs.
- Start the CD-burning software that is installed.
- Select "Burn a Data Disk" from the options displayed.
- Select the option "Disk at Once" if prompted.
- Select the disk format as ISO 9660 format if prompted.
- Click and drag the portfolio folder to the box in the burn CD window.
- Insert a blank CD-R disk.
- Push the "Burn" button or select "Burn" from the pull-down menu.

The capacity and relatively inexpensive pricing of CD-R media make this method of storage the most effective for most uses of e-portfolios. CD-R prices can, with some searching, be less than one dollar per disk and have been rumored to be as low as a half dollar per disk. Always be careful when labeling the disks so that neither the disk nor the coating of the disk is disturbed. It is recommended that you use a water-based marker (the organic solvents in most permanent markers may ruin the CD). If you use a labeling system to produce self-stick labels for the CD, ensure, as much as possible, that the label is centered appropriately, with no wrinkles or bubbles, before affixing it to the disk. It is important to identify the name of the program that will start the e-portfolio presentation. Should your e-portfolio include extensive graphics, music, or movies, you may exceed the capacity of the CD. In these cases, it may be necessary for you to use a disk with a larger capacity—a disk that uses more compressed data and both sides. You may need to save your material to a DVD.

❖ SAVING INFORMATION TO A DVD

Previous to several years ago, the term *DVD* was unknown to most people. DVD means digital versatile (also known as video) disk and has been widely used for the distribution of commercial movies. In the same way that the format of commercial music CDs is not compatible for use in saving data, commercial DVD formats, such as those that present movies, are not compatible with the kind of data storage that is needed for e-portfolio development. The e-portfolio author is advised strongly that the burning of a DVD requires that all artifacts as well as the PowerPoint presentation be located in a single folder. In most DVD-burning equipment, the DVD is inserted into the burner and prepared for burning, and the folder containing the information that the author wants saved is simply dragged to the DVD. Programs such as iDVD or Cinemaster are not necessary for most operations but represent options for advanced e-portfolio authors. The indexing and layout made available by programs such as iDVD and Cinemaster create a presentation that is as graphically appealing as a commercial movie DVD. Explaining how and providing directions to complete a DVD project made in a program such as iDVD or Cinemaster, however, are beyond the scope of this book. In general terms, follow these steps below to burn a DVD:

- Create a folder in "My Documents" or on the hard drive.
- Move all artifact files into the folder.
- Move the PowerPoint-based electronic portfolio into the folder.
- Run the PowerPoint to ensure that all hyperlinks work.
- Insert the DVD-R into the disk drive.
- When the DVD-R is formatted, an icon will appear.
- Drag the folder containing the portfolio files to the DVD-R icon.
- Select "Burn DVD" from the pull-down menu or drag to the trash.

There are a variety of DVDs on the market that can be used for recording. The DVD-R (recordable) disk recorder and reader is the most common of these and accounts, by some estimates, for up to nearly 80% of the market. Other types include DVD-RW (rewritable), which can be totally erased and then recorded again. There are also "video" versions, with some improvements that are not noticeable for most DVD uses. These DVD-R and DVD-RW are on the market but are hardware dependent. The DVD RAM is a version of the DVD that can be used for the temporary storage of files. However, given the inexpensive availability of hard drives, it seems too much like overkill to use a DVD for temporary purposes. It seems much more practical to use a hard drive for this purpose. Given the popularity and reasonable prices associated with the DVD-R, this type of DVD seems appropriate for the purposes of e-portfolio development.

DVD media are relatively more expensive than CD-R media. The most commonly used DVD media are the "general-purpose" DVD-R. Prices for DVD media do vary from store to store but can be expected to be about $4 each. Given the capacity to store large amounts of data, however, the price seems justified. The other types of DVD disks are more expensive and less used in practice. It is possible that the future will bring some interesting developments, including 9.4-gigabyte double-sided DVDs with data stored on both sides of the disk. For economic reasons and for issues of utility, it seems that the DVD-R is the practical choice for now.

SUMMARY

In this chapter, we discussed the common tools that should be available to the e-portfolio author. These tools include scanners, digital cameras, digital video cameras, and digitizers. Images are captured by digitizing spots of color called dots and displayed on monitors by blending tiny spots of color called pixels. The relationship of dots and pixels, as well as the sizes (640×480 dpi and 1024×768 pixels are recommended minimums) required by e-portfolio authors, was discussed. Saving these files on the same media outside of the hard drive would require a large amount of memory. As a result of this need for portable memory, a discussion of CD and DVD technology is found at the end of the chapter. It is recommended that CD-R or DVD-R technology be used, as they are the most common formats. Using these tools, the e-portfolio author is capable of producing quality artifacts that can be saved and distributed as portable, yet economically realistic, media.

QUESTIONS TO GUIDE E-PORTFOLIO PREPARATION

1. Identify what scanner technology to which you have access and classify it as one of three specific types of scanners.

2. Identify the name, image size possible, and how images are downloaded from a digital camera to which you have access.

3. Identify from "My Computer," under "View System Information" and within "Hardware," what CD or DVD capabilities to which you have access.

4. What is the best use for CD-RW technology, and why is distribution best for CD-R technology?

5. What is the major difference for e-portfolio authors when considering use of CD-R or DVD-R technology?

10

Special Considerations and Options

Focus Questions

- How have earlier chapters combined to enable an author to write an e-portfolio?
- What are common error patterns observed while authoring and viewing e-portfolios?
- Must one buy MS Office to view a PowerPoint-based e-portfolio?
- How can a PowerPoint presentation be moved to the Web?
- What developments expected in the future will affect e-portfolio development?

❖ INTRODUCTION

The e-portfolio requires advanced planning. In earlier chapters, the suggestions for producing an outline and using storyboards to guide development were provided in some detail. Because the primary function of the e-portfolio is to demonstrate that learning has taken place, the importance of reflection was emphasized. It is the reflection in which the author presents the basis for understanding how the standard is being read and how the standard is being met. Hyperlinking artifacts to each of the reflections becomes the means to establish that the assertions made in the reflections are actually occurring in practice.

This chapter will discuss the common errors, simple and perhaps more complex, that are made by e-portfolio authors. All of this is to ensure that the work that is put into e-portfolio development represents the author well in an operating finished product. Imagine that an e-portfolio is presented by a teacher candidate to a committee of faculty to establish that a teacher candidate meets the expectations of the preparing program. Imagine that that during the examination of the e-portfolio, the faculty committee cannot successfully link to artifacts or that artifacts cannot be read by the computer to which the committee has access. Even if the e-portfolio is designed and built in an exemplary fashion, if it does not run, the author needs to be proactive and solve the problem or problems before the e-portfolio is presented.

Following the discussion of error patterns, the chapter will present a short section to address the issue of saving the presentation in a form that is Web-friendly. There are some advantages to mounting all or some portion of the e-portfolio to the Web. The chapter concludes with a section that speculates about the future of computers in education, generally, and the future of e-portfolios as an assessment device.

❖ PLANNING AN E-PORTFOLIO

The success of your e-portfolio is due, in large part, to the time that you invest in planning the e-portfolio's development. The most common source of error in e-portfolio development is a lack of planning. As outlined in the first section of the book, a set of standards by which the author will demonstrate what he or she knows and is able to do is a first step in the development of the e-portfolio. That set of standards is the driving force behind the rest of the process. This is true whether the e-portfolio is being developed by preservice teachers to demonstrate that they meet their program's standards or by candidates for a teaching position to demonstrate that they can best perform their duties in the classroom. The successful candidate will present his or her beliefs, perhaps aligned with the widely accepted Interstate New Teacher Assessment and Support Consortium (INTASC) standards, but what is more, the successful candidate will present evidence that the beliefs are put into action.

Unlike paper-and-pencil portfolios, the e-portfolio author will present evidence in a variety of forms that may include documents, photographs, and video. An e-portfolio of evidence can be created without standards to serve as an organizational device, yet nothing can be done with such an e-portfolio that cannot be done with a physical collection of artifacts in a binder or box. The e-portfolio is useful only when the standards and artifacts are able to interact with each other to provide the viewer with the evidence that requirements or standards are met. The e-portfolio serves, then, as a mechanism that can be used for assessment purposes. The e-portfolio reflections of each standard are read, and then the viewer reacts to the artifacts in terms of their abilities to demonstrate that the standards are met. Without these characteristics, a collection of work samples is just that and no more.

The second decision that needs to be made in the development of an e-portfolio is to determine the purpose the e-portfolio will serve (see Chapter 2). The selection of artifacts should emerge from the purpose of the e-portfolio so that the coherence of the e-portfolio is evident to the viewer. The reflections and self-assessment pieces tie all of the artifacts and other elements of the e-portfolio to the purpose. It is in the reflections where the teachers and students demonstrate that they are critical thinkers and understand what the performance standards mean. It is best to draw an image of how the e-portfolio will be structured and how the artifacts will be hyperlinked both to the reflections and to each other. Hyperlinking is outlined in Chapter 8. Once the standards are known and understood, the purpose of the e-portfolio is clearly established, and the basic structure of the e-portfolio is outlined, the process of digitizing all of the artifacts is the next step.

Digitizing the artifacts involves using a group of tools that are outlined in Chapter 8 and include both tools and programs. The use of digital cameras, scanners, digital video cameras, and digitizers is reviewed in Chapter 8. The use of the Adobe PhotoShop program is also reviewed in Chapter 9 to ensure that all artifacts are of a quality that will speak well for the e-portfolio and, therefore, the e-portfolio developer. Thus, any kind of artifact that might be placed within a physical portfolio is possible for inclusion in an e-portfolio as a digitized artifact. Photographs are scanned, lesson or strategic plans can be in word-processing files, and teaching sequences or seminar presentations can be included as digital video captured directly by digital video cameras or from standard VHS through a digitizer. It should be remembered that, unlike a physical portfolio, the digital files can be related to each other through creative linking. A word-processed strategic plan can be hyperlinked to a digital file, which may be a speech that outlines the plan to a company's employees. This is a characteristic that really sets the e-portfolio apart from its physical counterparts.

Once the artifacts are digitized, the PowerPoint presentation should be composed, beginning with a title page and a table of contents. An appropriate font and a slide background need to be selected that will serve to highlight but not upstage the presentation. The PowerPoint presentation should present each standard or requirement followed by a reflection. The PowerPoint presentation ends with a page of acknowledgments to recognize the permissions that were received from those who contributed to the e-portfolio. Once the general framework is in place, the hyperlinks should be inserted into the PowerPoint presentation to internally link the slides to each other in a way that makes sense. Then, hyperlinks are inserted to provide a pathway for viewing the digitized artifacts selected for inclusion in the e-portfolio. This is when the PowerPoint e-portfolio has advantages that are not present in the physical collection. The ability to link one artifact to another related artifact, which is used to address another related standard, is a real advantage. Remember that not all files are PowerPoint-friendly (the process of hyperlinking is described in Chapter 8, and a list of compatible file types is provided in Figure 8.2).

Once the PowerPoint presentation has been completed, it should be saved and then tested. It must be remembered that the artifacts and the PowerPoint e-portfolio presentation must be saved to the same single folder before hyperlinks are established. In this way, the author can be sure that the hyperlinks will "point" or "jump" to the correct files. If the PowerPoint presentation is not saved in the same folder as the artifacts, then there will be difficulties in establishing the "pathways" that describe how the hyperlinks will browse once the presentation and artifacts are taken to a computer different from the one on which it was authored. If the PowerPoint hyperlinks, for example, point to files that are saved separately (e.g., in a folder on your computer's hard drive), then the hyperlink may look for the file through the pathway "HD/user/DAW Documents/EarthScience/LessonPlans/Rocksintro .doc." This pathway describes a file called "Rocksintro.doc," which is found within a folder called "LessonPlans." That folder is found, in turn, in a folder called "EarthScience," which is in the "Documents" folder on this particular computer's hard drive on a space reserved for "DAW." When this PowerPoint presentation is saved, along with the artifacts, to a CD and transferred to a different computer, then since no space is reserved for a user called "DAW" on the new computer's hard drive, the hyperlink will fail to operate. This is because the pathway describes a set of files on a different computer that is now inaccessible. The PowerPoint hyperlink would simply fail with an error message. Should this happen during an e-portfolio assessment, it would speak ill of the presentation author. Thus, care needs to be taken regarding how the files are saved, and care also must be taken to test the presentation.

❖ WHAT HAPPENED? A GUIDE TO
   COMMON TECHNICAL ERRORS

The frustrating experiences of many have gone into the writing of this section. We would like to thank our many students who, like us, have found the initial attempts at developing e-portfolios both educational and trying. The common errors fall into two categories: hardware and software problems. Only a few of the difficulties are discussed here, and not all of the problems have answers that work all of the time. This book has attempted to discuss the processes of e-portfolio development across platforms and across applications. We discuss the problems with these processes in this section. Complicating the task of troubleshooting a troublesome presentation is the PowerPoint software itself. PowerPoint is constantly being updated, but versions exist that are quite dated yet still routinely used. Will this section speak to all versions of PowerPoint, all versions of tools that are used, all hardware platforms, or all levels of users? It is unlikely. What this section will do is point to a few basic error patterns that have been observed.

Error observed: CD, DVD will not "run," cannot be found, or will not display as an option as a PowerPoint presentation "on a computer other than the one on which it was authored."

The most common error in this event is the format in which the presentation has been saved. If a presentation is created on a Macintosh computer and the disk is transferred to a Windows-based computer, the presentation may not run. In this event, the presentation and all of the files must be saved in a Windows-friendly format and all artifact files named with an appropriate extension (.doc, .xls, .ppt, .jpg, etc.). If a CD-R is burned using a Windows-only format, the presentation may not run on a Macintosh. If a CD-R is formatted to read only on Macintosh platforms, it will not run on Windows-based computers. If a DVD+R disk and recorder are used to save the presentation, the DVD will not "run" on a computer that has the more common DVD-R reader. Thus, if the presentation will not "run," check the format of the presentation, as well as the extensions used on the files that are serving as both the e-portfolio and the artifacts. In addition, ensure that the CD is burned in a format required by the computer on which the presentation is to be "run" or in a format that is friendly to the majority of computers equipped with CD drives (ISO 9660).

Error observed: The PowerPoint disk generates a warning from the computer that the disk is not readable or that the disk needs to be formatted.

This is the same error as above. The format in which the disk was created is not compatible with the computer being used. Under no circumstances should the viewer choose to reformat the disk, as all saved information will be lost. Instead, return the disk to the same machine on which it was created, retrieve all of the files to a folder on the hard drive, insert appropriate media, and save the folder to this new media. Macintosh users are encouraged to save the final products to Windows-friendly media and in ISO 9660 format since Windows-based computers are the norm in many instances. Fortunately, most computers are burning CD-R media in ISO 9660 formats as the default setting. This development alone will eliminate a major source of confusion for e-portfolio authors.

Error observed: PowerPoint-based e-portfolio slides are difficult to navigate as animation makes it difficult to know when the information on a slide is completely displayed.

The use of the slide transition for the first several slides of a PowerPoint-based e-portfolio may well be appropriate. As the viewer moves from the title to the table of contents, for example, the effects of the slide transition may be welcomed. However, requiring the viewer to click through the information on a title slide or any slide containing a bulleted list, for example, is usually unwelcome. For those cases in which animation may be appropriate (the title slide, for example), establish the animation to change through careful timing rather than requiring a mouse click. The navigation will be made easier this way, and the viewer will recognize when it is safe to click the hyperlinks. In addition, remember that when returning to the table of contents, if animation is established, the animation will show each time the viewer returns to that table. Animation, in that case, wastes time that just may be the viewer's most precious commodity.

Error message: Cannot open the specified file.

The first and most obvious error made when this warning appears is that the file pathway is wrong. During the creation of the hyperlink, for instance, it may be that the file was identified during "browsing" as being located on the author's hard drive rather than from the correct location being the single folder in which the artifacts and the PowerPoint-based e-portfolio were to be saved. The presentation, therefore, is "looking" to a file that is no longer with the disk. For example, the file may be a particular lesson plan saved both on a teacher candidate's laptop computer and also in the single folder that was to be later burned to a CD-R. However, during browsing and subsequent identification of that lesson plan, the location of the plan was identified as the hard drive/documents/plan folder rather than a location relative only to the folder containing all files that were to be burned. The PowerPoint presentation may very well "run" on the author's computer because that computer does have the file described by the pathway identifying that specific file on that specific laptop. Move the burned disk to another computer, however, and the pathway of the original computer fails to work, and the file cannot be found let alone be opened. The pathway would have to be changed, with the revised PowerPoint presentation saved and then written (or burned) onto new media.

A second source of this error is a document saved in the wrong format. A Macintosh-created MS Word document may not be saved with the Windows-required extension. If a Windows-based computer looks at a file called "lesson plan," the computer may not recognize it as an MS Word document. It lacks the extension ".doc" on the end of the filename. An additional source of this problem is a file not compatible with PowerPoint. Although MP3 sound files are perfectly compatible, WAVE sound files are not and would result in the same error message. Therefore, on a Windows-based computer, when a hyperlink to such a file is activated, the file will not be recognized and simply will not open. The error message, in its graphic honesty, is more damaging than the error itself. This kind of error warrants the extra time to correct the file format or name, correct the hyperlink, and then make a new copy of the entire folder on new (or rewritten) media.

Finally, a third error source may be in identifying the destination for the hyperlink on older computers. If a full hyperlink is used to identify the specific drive, the specific media source, and the specific folder for a hyperlinked file, it is possible that another computer may use a different drive or naming convention that could render the link useless. The use of a *relative pathway* can avoid this error pattern by identifying the file by its unique name rather than a specific location. These errors can be corrected by reestablishing the link with *action settings*, with the *relative pathway* option selected where relative pathways are not default, but must be selected with a check box on the hyperlink pop-up window.

Error message: Could not find the application that created the document (portfolio name). To open the document, select an alternate program, with or without translation.

It is possible, especially when creating an e-portfolio on a computer other than the computer that will be used to view the PowerPoint presentation, that a different version of PowerPoint will be used. It is important to identify the file that is the e-portfolio and to do that both with the name of the file and with instructions on the media used. If the e-portfolio is saved to a CD-R, then it may be possible to create a label complete with instructions on which file is to be accessed. The placement of the label is critical, and some companies sell a small machine that assists in placing the label. It may be more practical just to use a water-based marker to identify the file of interest. Remember that bubbles under a label, an off-center label, or a label that is wrinkled may render a CD or DVD unreadable. Simply identify that the file named "myportfolio.ppt" should be opened with Microsoft PowerPoint.

To assist with identifying the difficulties encountered in running PowerPoint-based e-portfolios, we have provided a very basic troubleshooting guide in the appendix. This may assist the frustrated developer in identifying the nature of the observed problems. The likely reason for each problem, as well as a suggested remedy, is provided within the guide.

❖ DOWNLOADING REQUIRED PROGRAMS—FOR FREE

Microsoft Corporation recognizes the widespread use of PowerPoint as a tool for the dissemination of information. As a corporation, it has activated a site that will allow any computer user to download a PowerPoint reader for free. This is a version of PowerPoint that cannot be used to author a presentation—that would require the purchase of the program separately or, more commonly, as a part of the Microsoft Office Suite in one form or another. To expect a potential assessor of a candidate to buy and install a copy of Microsoft Office Suite is unrealistic. A free download, however, is a more reasonable possibility. The Internet address for such free downloads is as follows: http://microsoft.com/downloads/. On this site, it is possible to identify the computer hardware being used and to download the appropriate reader for use on the system. It is advisable to include directions for downloading the reader with the distribution of the PowerPoint-based e-portfolio. If the presentation is being distributed as a CD or a DVD, then it may be possible to write these instructions (and even the "open with application" instructions outlined above) as an insert into the disk case in which the e-portfolio is to be distributed. Like the information that accompanies your favorite music CD, perhaps instructions would replace lyrics and band pictures.

The steps for downloading the reader are relatively simple. Go to the Microsoft download center at microsoft.com/downloads/search.asx?DisplayLang=en and follow these steps:

- Enter "PowerPoint Viewer" in the keywords box.
- Navigate to the download center for PowerPoint Viewer.
- Select from the versions of PowerPoint according to your operating system and hardware.
- Click on the appropriate version to go to the download screen.
- Click on "Download."

The download will be saved to your computer, and the PowerPoint Viewer can be used to examine any PowerPoint presentation, all without cost. A model of suggested wording to be customized and included with any distributed PowerPoint-based e-portfolio is provided for your consideration in Figure 10.1.

❖ DOWNLOADING QUICKTIME—FOR FREE

Many e-portfolios developed on Windows-based platforms may not run smoothly on Macintosh OS-based machines without the addition of the Windows Media Player. Photos, video snippets, movies, and even some scanned documents may require this technology to be able to decode the compression used to save the files. Thus, Windows

Figure 10.1   Model "Read Me First" Language for Inclusion With an
Electronic Portfolio

Welcome to the Portfolio of John Q. Public. Within this portfolio, I shall respond to all standards as established by the Interstate New Teacher Assessment and Support Consortium. The portfolio is a PowerPoint-based product. Follow these instructions to view the portfolio.

1. Insert the CD into the CD drive of your computer.

2. Browse to the CD and open the CD entitled "John Q. Public Portfolio."

3. Double click on the file named "JQPublicPortfolio.ppt."

4. If the file does not automatically open but asks for the application to be used, select the version of PowerPoint or PowerPoint Viewer that is installed on your computer.

5. You may then view the slide show and use the buttons (or highlighted terms) to navigate through the presentation.

6. This portfolio is being made available to you for the purpose of obtaining employment and, due to the sensitive nature of some artifacts, may not be distributed or shared beyond this purpose.

7. Remember to use the navigation aids as you view the portfolio.

If you do not have PowerPoint or a PowerPoint Viewer, you may download a free version of PowerPoint Viewer by following the steps below:

1. Using your Internet browser, go to the Microsoft download center at "microsoft.com/downloads/search.asx?DisplayLang=en."

2. In the keyword box, search by entering "PowerPoint Viewer."

3. This will take you to a page that will display the various versions of the program.

4. Select the version of PowerPoint Viewer that is consistent with your hardware equipment and disk operating system.

5. Confirm your choice by reviewing the hardware requirements that will be displayed.

6. Click on "Download."

7. You may then open the PowerPoint Viewer to open and view my portfolio.

Media Player will have to be downloaded using the following directions.

- Using your Web browser, go to www.microsoft.com/windows/ windowsmedia/download/.
- Select the appropriate version given the operating system of your computer.
- Select the appropriate language.
- Read the conditions and click on "Download Now."

Similarly, e-portfolios developed on Macintosh OS-based platforms may not run smoothly on a Windows-based machine. Thus, QuickTime technology may be required to open the images, video snippets, or movies within the PowerPoint-based e-portfolio. Like the Microsoft Corporation and its PowerPoint program and Windows Media Player, the authors of QuickTime, the Apple Corporation, have enabled a site for free downloads. This program can be downloaded to most Macintosh and Windows-based computers using the following directions:

- Using your Web browser, go to www.apple.com/quicktime/ products/qt/.
- If you wish to install QuickTime, choose "Download QuickTime."
- Select the platform and the operating system of your computer.
- Click on "Download."

Providing these directions to a viewer in a "Read Me First" file is strongly advised when an e-portfolio may cross platform boundaries.

❖ THE TOP 10 LIST

To paraphrase late-night television, this list comes directly from the authors' home base in Scranton, Pennsylvania. It is composed of the top 10 most frequent errors that e-portfolio authors have made over the past several years. They are platform independent but always result in unsatisfactory products. Perhaps it is a list, organized from number 1 being experienced in the initial e-portfolio authoring decision to number 10 being the last step before using the e-portfolio. Perhaps you can use it to review your work. The Top 10 List focuses on you, as an e-portfolio author, and is presented on the next page:

The PowerPoint e-portfolio author has . . .

1. Failed to select a set of standards appropriate to the use of the e-portfolio

2. Failed to reflect deeply or to represent that reflection well in the writing

3. Failed to select appropriate artifact files to demonstrate that the reflection is accurate in practice

4. Failed to limit artifact filenames to eight characters (excluding extensions)

5. Failed to place the PowerPoint e-portfolio and all artifacts in the same folder previous to beginning the hyperlinking process

6. Failed to hyperlink to the correct file since multiple copies of the e-portfolio and artifact files exist, causing confusion as to which copy is inside the correct folder

7. Failed to recognize contributions of others (including images in photos and video snippets or student work) or maintain permissions received for their use

8. Did not include a "Read Me First" file to identify and then describe how the e-portfolio is navigated

9. Did not describe, within "Read Me First," which programs might need to be downloaded and from what source

10. Failed to test the e-portfolio presentation on different computers with various operating systems

❖ MOVING A POWERPOINT PRESENTATION TO THE WEB

In the first half of the book, and again in Chapter 6, it is pointed out that among all of the e-portfolio tools available, PowerPoint was chosen for this book as a platform on which to construct e-portfolios. There may be reasons to save the e-portfolio PowerPoint presentation in HyperText Markup Language (HTML), the language of the World Wide Web. Perhaps your teacher preparation program requires the mounting of your e-portfolio to a departmental server for assessment. Perhaps you are not sure what program you will be expected to use when presenting the e-portfolio and you wish to have the option to import it as a presentation on one of many presentation software packages. However, there are also many limitations to this process, and there is limited space in this book available to outline these. Thus, the following discussion will be more brief than complete, and more of an outline to achieve an end that is not necessarily intended by the authors of a book using PowerPoint as the means.

PowerPoint comes complete with a useful feature that can be used during the saving process. From the "File" pull-down menu, selecting "Save As" will cause a pop-up box to open. This has been reviewed earlier in the text. The PowerPoint presentation can be saved as an HTML file simply be indicating that objective by changing the "Save as File Type" window in the pop-up box.

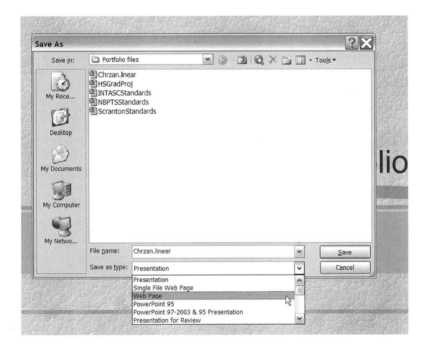

The entire presentation will be converted to HTML and saved with that indication as an extension. If you opt to save your PowerPoint e-portfolio file as HTML, you should be aware of several limitations. These limitations will have to be addressed before saving the file as HTML. A consideration of the limitations, as well as possible answers to those limitations, is provided on the next page.

Among the limitations that you will experience is a loss of the animation that may be present in the PowerPoint presentation. This includes slide transition and animation. When a person visits a Web site, it is a distraction to see slide transitions or too much animation anyway. In addition, those features would act to slow the performance of the Web browser. In addition, hyperlinking should be eliminated since hyperlinking on the Web, while similar in principle, will be different when the presentation is mounted to the Web. Therefore, task number one is to eliminate all of that clutter in order to save what is really important; the standards and reflections. Use the "Action Setting" under the "Slide Show" pull-down menu to erase hyperlinks, and use the delete key to eliminate buttons as necessary.

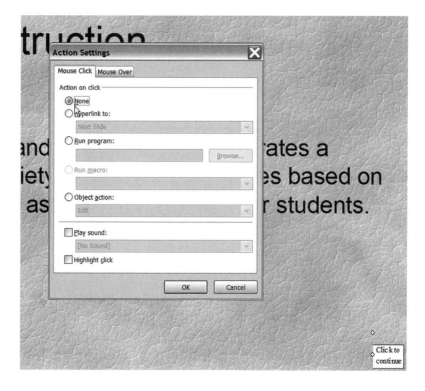

As part of the planning process, you will have a clear record of what file goes with what reflection, so it is important to remember that restoring the hyperlinks in the HTML format will not present a big challenge.

Once you have the PowerPoint saved in HTML, you will want to save each of the artifact document photo files as a separate page in HTML language by changing the format to Web-friendly versions. This is done in a manner similar to the way in which the PowerPoint file was saved by using the "Web Page" selection from the "Save as File Type" window in the "Save As" pop-up box. Videos, movies, and photos will not have to be converted. Follow the instructions below to create hyperlinks to these files.

You will have to create text boxes (an option under the "Insert" pull-down menu) and write the intended destination inside the text box. Multiple text boxes can be used to create links, for example, to "back to the index," "Artifact 1," or "Artifact 2."

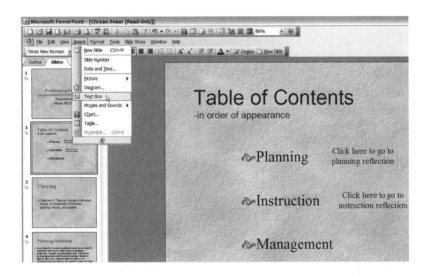

Highlight the intended test and then, under the "Insert" pull-down menu, select "Hyperlink." From the hyperlink pop-up box, hyperlink to a Web page, browse until you find the name of the appropriate file saved in HTML-friendly form, and save. You will know that the hyperlink is created when the text becomes underlined and is indicated in a different color.

Once the hyperlinks are established, the entire project should be mounted to an appropriate Web server. The selection of the server and the manner in which the Webmaster will mount the pages are clearly beyond the scope of this work. Editing the Web page is not much

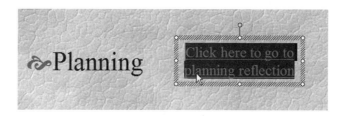

different from editing a PowerPoint presentation. It is simply a matter of downloading the file, changing the hyperlink or editing the writing, and having the Web material uploaded to the Web server again.

❖ THE FUTURE: WHAT PROMISES TO MAKE
ELECTRONIC PORTFOLIOS MORE EFFECTIVE?

One of the most amazing facts to consider is how complex computers have become over the past several decades. Many of us celebrated when we owned our first personal computer. For some of us, it was a Commodore Vic20 with about 7.5K of RAM. For others, it may have been a TRS-80, an integrated IBM-clone CPU monitor unit that bragged about its 128K of memory. How many of us remember adding a "sider" external hard drive to our Apple IIe systems to more efficiently use the 32-megahertz (MHz) speed of the machine and store the results of our use of the computer's 128K memory? Now computer memory is measured in gigabytes, and servers are measured in terabytes. Speed has increased dramatically and is typically measured in home computers in terms of the gigahertz. What a change from the early computers slogging around at 32 MHz.

Even home computers, especially those in homes where graphics are important (computer gamers, for example), use wildly powerful computers. The resolution of large graphics files requires speeds where the target of performance approaches instantaneous, and the ability to download Internet information is now limited by communications hardware and not computer speed. This blazing speed is one of the areas that will continue to expand in the future. As discussed in Chapter 9, the 10-gigabyte storage capability of double-sided DVDs is an idea nearing obsolescence where they too will join the once essential floppy drives. The time lapse between hyperlinking to documents, images, and video that can now be seen with many types of media and media drives will become a thing of the past as media capacity, volume, and drive speed continue to increase.

The assessment of professional educators is sure to continue changing, and perhaps increasingly in response to a performance-based revolution we have seen in recent years. Perhaps the instantaneous e-portfolio—possibly mind driven—may be a standard of the future. Perhaps with the kind of volume and speed made possible with future development, the standard for e-portfolios may become virtual reality displays, and assessment may be based on what the candidate is thinking rather than what they are saying or writing. Can you imagine a new test program emanating from the large psychometric corporations where, instead of grading responses to questions of a test, the candidate is strapped inside a virtual reality suit, and responses to virtually real situations are graded on the basis of actual movement or thought patterns? Imagine that physical challenges and even those disabilities that interfere with performance on pencil-and-paper tests would all be moot. The limitations of the disabilities could be measured in terms of the actual work expectations, and the ability of a disabled person to work within the limits of reasonable accommodation could be clearly demonstrated. That may be the stuff of *Star Trek,* but so were talking computers.

In the old days of the not so distant past, PowerPoint also has developed in a number of ways. The capacity for including a larger number of graphics and special effects is just one indication. The ability to insert, adjust, and customize external files is sure to increase. Another development will be the "feel" of the program as we run it on our computers. Although there was nothing wrong with the older versions of PowerPoint, newer versions are more user-friendly and offer the user evermore clear directions on its use. Just one look, as an example, at Microsoft PowerPoint 2007 is a sneak peek at the future. It is there where files are saved in similar formats, and hyperlinking does not need to start up word-processing or spreadsheet programs in order to simply view an existing file. Performance in that environment is increased dramatically, and the RAM of the computer in use is not challenged.

The e-portfolio, in its many iterations, is a strong beginning for where performance assessment needs to go. The specific example outlined in this text, the PowerPoint-based e-portfolio, lacks a feature that needs to be developed in the future. If 10 candidates for a communications degree all meet the standard, then it should be possible to download all of the candidates' artifacts separately into massively interactive databases. Database sizes are already expanding as storage components grow exponentially. Imagine a university communications program with the power to demonstrate to prospective students the kinds of student performances that their program generates within one particular standard area. Some companies already use a somewhat limited form of interactive database as they save e-portfolio artifacts into rigidly designed Web-based e-portfolios. It is reasonable to expect that the future will allow those communications students to identify in their e-portfolios with a code as to which artifacts are directly related to a mass-media production standard, for example, and have all 10 graduates' related artifacts mined as a distinct file from the e-portfolio files. For the purposes of program evaluation, which increasingly cries for accountability, as well as for more traditional accreditation reports, this would be a giant step forward.

Finally, experience indicates that students and job candidates are much more willing to learn and respond to performance assessment through e-portfolio construction than are key people in decision making to review e-portfolios in an electronic format. In the future, it is possible that position searches and job opportunities will be announced in terms that will require the submission of e-portfolios. This may be the most daunting task that faces those of us involved in performance assessment, for the decision makers need to be educated regarding how these requirements or standards can be written and how the e-portfolios of the present and the future can be accessed. The most striking e-portfolio can describe the most ideal candidate, but all is for naught if the interviewer does not or cannot take the time to view the e-portfolio. This is true whether discussing academic program completion, the review of candidate e-portfolios, or evaluation processes, perhaps including rank and tenure at colleges and universities. With an e-portfolio, the interviewer could navigate in short order each candidate's artifacts in the requirement or standard thought to be most important. Yet there must be a certain facility of the e-portfolio reviewer in the running of the programs and the assessment of e-portfolios. In the future, perhaps, as this computer-literate and hyperlink-skilled generation replaces those of us from a bygone overhead projector era, this will be a challenge that disappears through attrition.

The promise of e-portfolios is too great to allow matters of preparation to interfere with implementation. Perhaps this book has moved us forward an inch or two.

SUMMARY

This chapter has reviewed the basic elements of earlier chapters to show how the second half of this work combines with the first to enable an author to compose a PowerPoint-based e-portfolio. This extended from selecting PowerPoint as an authoring tool (Chapter 6), composing a basic PowerPoint presentation (Chapter 7), making the e-portfolio less linear through the use of hyperlinks (Chapter 8), using common ancillary tools that enable the development of high-quality artifact files (Chapter 9), and analyzing error patterns in the PowerPoint-based e-portfolio presentation itself (this chapter). The book is directional, taking the reader from the "why" to the "how" of PowerPoint-based e-portfolios.

This chapter also discussed options to mount PowerPoint e-portfolios to the Web with a basic outline of required changes to save the file in appropriate formats. Reasons to do this were discussed, and routes to address the limitations were suggested.

The chapter then addressed improvements that have been made in the PowerPoint program and speculated on how future improvements in technology may affect the e-portfolio author. Higher computer and media-driven operating speeds, higher memory capacities, and programs with more numerous features may all make the e-portfolio of the future much different. Perhaps the future may see the e-portfolio stored on media and played in a manner that creates a virtual reality for the viewer. For the time being, however, the creative capacity of an e-portfolio author can be maximized, and security issues can be minimized, through the use of PowerPoint-based e-portfolios.

QUESTIONS TO GUIDE E-PORTFOLIO PREPARATION

1. Describe how an e-portfolio with poorly written reflections but excellent artifacts may not be assessed as well as an e-portfolio with excellent reflections and poorly presented artifacts.

2. You are proofreading a classmate's e-portfolio, and when you select an artifact that is a digital photograph, an error message flashes telling that the image cannot be displayed. Suggest what may be required to correct the error.

3. In viewing an e-portfolio, your attempt to link to an MS Word file results in an error message that the file cannot be located. Suggest why that may have occurred.

4. Where can you find free copies of PowerPoint Reader, Windows Media Player, and QuickTime?

5. Identify a person to whom you need to present appropriately edited files to have them uploaded to the Web and where the Web server is located.

6. Speculate as to why a school superintendent might prefer to see results of a situational-based virtual reality test rather than a series of pencil-and-paper tests.

7. How would assessment through virtual reality address the individual differences of several types of physically and cognitively challenged teacher candidates?

Appendix

Troubleshooting Your PowerPoint-Based E-Portfolio

Insert the media containing the errant PowerPoint-based e-portfolio into the computer and follow the choices in the dichotomous key found below:

1a. The PowerPoint e-portfolio file cannot be found (go to 2).
1b. The PowerPoint e-portfolio file can be found and "run" (go to 3).

2a. The PowerPoint e-portfolio presentation fails when tried on most other computers.
   • The PowerPoint e-portfolio is in a format not recognized by the computer.
   • Return the media to the original computer and save in a different format.
2b. The PowerPoint e-portfolio cannot be found among the files when listed.
   • The PowerPoint may reside outside the single folder for the e-portfolio.
   • Move the e-portfolio file inside the folder and reestablish hyperlinks.

3a. The PowerPoint e-portfolio presentation runs but links will not work (go to 4).
3b. The PowerPoint e-portfolio presentation opens but is difficult to navigate.
   • Presentation requires too many clicks, or hyperlinks are not clearly identified.
   • More clearly identify how to hyperlink and/or eliminate the need for clicking.

4a. The PowerPoint e-portfolio hyperlink causes an error message (go to 5).

4b. The PowerPoint e-portfolio hyperlink does not do anything.
- The hyperlink does not define a target file or Web page.
- Revise the hyperlink destination using "Action Settings" under the "Slide Show" pull-down menu or "Hyperlink" under the "Insert" pull-down menu.

5a. The PowerPoint hyperlink should be checked to ensure file location and name.
- The hyperlink may point to a file location not accessible by the computer.
- The filename may have been truncated, resulting in it having a different name.
- Move the file to a location that is accessible or reestablish the hyperlink using a new name.

5b. The PowerPoint hyperlink should be checked for the appropriate extension.
- The hyperlink may point to a file without a mandatory extension.
- Revise the filename to include the extension required.
- The file may have to be edited to use a PowerPoint-friendly format.

References

Amen, K., Keogh, T., & Wolff, N. (2002). Digital copyright: A tale of domestic discord, presented in three acts. *Computers in Libraries, 22*, 22–27.

Anthony, R., & Roe, G. (2002). *The curriculum vitae handbook: How to present and promote your academic career.* San Francisco: Rudi Publications.

Barrett, H. (2000). *How to create your own electronic portfolio.* Retrieved August 19, 2007, from electronic portfolios.com Web site: http://electronicportfolios.com/portfolios/howto/index.html

Birkeland, S., Johnson, S. M., Kardos, S. M., Kauffman, D., Liu, E., & Peske, H. G. (2001, July). Retaining the next generation of teachers. *Harvard School of Education Newsletter.* Retrieved June 20, 2003, from www.edletter.org/past/issues/2001-ja/support.shtml

Bondy, E., & Ross, D. (2005). *Preparing for inclusive teaching: Meeting the challenges of teacher education reform.* Albany: State University of New York Press.

Bruner, J. (1966). *Toward a theory of instruction.* Cambridge, MA: Harvard University Press.

Campbell, D. M., Melenyzer, B. J., Nettles, D. H., & Wyman, R. M., Jr. (2000). *Portfolio and performance assessment in teacher education.* Boston: Allyn & Bacon.

College media group cautions that 2 copyright laws could collide. (2003). *Chronicle of Higher Education, 49*(29), A29.

Darling-Hammond, L., Ancess, J., & Falk, B. (1995). *Authentic assessment in action: Studies of schools and students at work.* New York: Teachers College Press.

Dewey, J. (1916). *Democracy and education.* New York: Free Press.

Dewey, J. (1933). *How we think.* Chicago: Henry Regnery.

Eby, J. (1997). *Reflective planning, teaching, and evaluation for the elementary school.* Upper Saddle River, NJ: Prentice Hall.

Flavell, J. (1985). *Cognitive development* (2nd ed.). Englewood Cliffs, NJ: Prentice Hall.

Grabe, C., & Grabe, M. (1998). *Integrating technology for meaningful learning.* New York: Houghton Mifflin.

Halverson, M. (2000). *This is a presenting solution! Web site: Hierarchy and contrast: The basis of good design.* Retrieved March 2003 from www.power pointers.com/showarticle.asp?articleid=399

Hebert, E. A. (2001). *The power of portfolios: What children can teach us about learning and assessment.* San Francisco: Jossey-Bass.

Hein, G., & Price, S. (1994). *Active assessment for active science.* Portsmouth, NH: Heinemann.

Kardos, S. M., & Liu, E. (2003, April 22). New research finds school hiring and support practices fall short. *Harvard Education Letter.* Retrieved June 2003 from www.gse.harvard.edu

Kendall, J., & Marzano, R. (1996). *Content knowledge: A compendium of standards and benchmarks for K–12 educators.* Aurora, CO: Mid-Continent Regional Educational Laboratory.

Kendall, J., & Marzano, R. (2004). *Content knowledge: A compendium of standards and benchmarks for K–12 education.* Aurora, CO: Mid-Continent Research for Education and Learning.

Lyons, N. (1998). Portfolios and their consequences: Developing as a reflective practitioner. In N. Lyons (Ed.), *With portfolio in hand: Validating the new teacher professionalism* (pp. 247–264). New York: Teachers College Press.

Martin-Kniep, G. (1997). Implementing authentic assessment in the classroom, school, and school district. In J. Cohen & R. Wiener (Eds.), *Literacy portfolios: Using assessment to guide instruction.* Upper Saddle River, NJ: Prentice Hall.

Montgomery, K. K. (2001). *Authentic assessment: A guide for elementary teachers.* New York: Allyn & Bacon.

National Association of State Directors of Teacher Education and Certification. (2000). *How the states respond to NBPTS-certified teachers.* Retrieved from www.nasdtec.org

National Commission on Excellence in Education. (1983). *A nation at risk: The imperative for educational reform.* Washington, DC: U.S. Department of Education.

Noam, E. M. (1997, October). *Will books become the dumb medium?* Keynote address to the Annual Convention of Educom, Minneapolis, MN.

Parkay, F. W., & Standford, B. H. (2004). *Becoming a teacher.* New York: Allyn & Bacon.

Piaget, J. (1973). *To understand is to invent.* New York: Grossman.

Schön, D. A. (1987). *Educating the reflective practitioner: Toward a new design for teaching and learning in the professions.* San Francisco: Jossey-Bass.

Seldin, P. (1997). *The teaching portfolio: A practical guide to improved performance and promotion/tenure decisions* (2nd ed.). Boston: Anker.

Shulman, L. (1987). Knowledge and teaching: Foundations of the new reform. *Harvard Educational Review, 57,* 1–22.

Sternberg, R. (1986). *Intelligence applied: Understanding and increasing your intellectual skills.* San Diego: Harcourt Brace Jovanovich.

Trigwell, K., Martin, E., & Benjamin, J. (2000). Scholarship of teaching: A model. *Higher Education Research and Development, 19,* 155–168.

U.S. Department of Education. (2002). *No Child Left Behind: A desktop reference.* Washington, DC: Author.

Warburton, E., & Torff, B. (2005). The effect of perceived learner advantages on teachers' beliefs about critical-thinking activities. *Journal of Teacher Education, 56,* 24–33.

Williams, R. (1994). *The non-designers book: Design and typographic principles for the visual novice.* Berkeley, CA: Peachpit Press.

Yost, M. (2000, February 3). Communicate with color. *WebReference Update Newsletter.* Retrieved May 2003 from www.webreference.com/new/color2.html

Zubizarreta, J. (1994). Teaching portfolios and the beginning teacher. *Phi Delta Kappan, 74,* 323–326.

Index

Academic portfolio, 23
Action button, for hyperlinks, 137
Action Setting, 200
Add Effect, 125
Adobe PhotoShop, 189
Adobe PhotoShop Elements,
    148, 174
Adobe Premiere, 159, 176
ALF files, 133
ALFF files, 133
Amen, K., 129
American Alliance for Health,
    Physical Education, Recreation
    and Dance, 57
American Council of Teachers of
    Foreign Language (ACTFL), 56
American Psychological Association
    (APA), 129
Animation, 123–125, 124*f*
Apple Cinema monitor, 169
Apple Extended format, 181
Apple Keynote, 104*t*
Arial font, 118
Artifacts
    defining, 6
    digitizing, 189–190
    sampling with Scranton
        model, 50*f*
    scanning, 168, 170–172
Assessment
    authentic, 6, 14
    defining, 6
    literacy, 15–16
    performance, 7
    portfolio, 7, 8–11
    standards for, 46, 53*f*, 55*f*
    vs. evaluation, 5–6

Assessment reflection, 68
Audio. *See* Sound
Authentic assessment, 6, 14
Authentic task, 4–5, 6
Auto-content wizard, 114

Barrett, Helen, 4
Benjamin, J., 23
Best-Work Evaluation Form, 73*f*
Bibliographic citations, 129, 131
A Bit Better Corporation, 78
Bondy, E., 62
Bruner, J., 12
Bulleted lists, 116, 123
Burning CD, 179–183

Category, in PowerPoint, 129
CD
    burning, 179–183
    CD-R, 179–180
    CD-R, cost of, 182
    CD-R, labeling, 194
    CD-RW, 180
    disk-at-once (DAO)
        recording, 182
Chalk and Wire electronic portfolio
    systems, 98
Chicago font, 118
Cinemaster, 183
Citations, bibliographic, 129, 131
Classroom portfolios, 35–41
    sample page, 36*f*
Classroom-based inquiry, 62
Clip art, 129–130
Cold Fusion, 105
Collaboration, ethics, and
    relationships reflection, 68–69

213

Collaboration with colleagues standards, 55*f*
College instructors, portfolios for, 25, 26
Comic sans font, 117
Communication and technology standards, 53*f*
Communication reflection, 68
Compression, 170
Consortium of National Arts Education Associations, 57
Constructivism, 3–4, 12, 62
Content description, problems with variations in, 44
Content knowledge, 62
Content organization, example, 40*f*
Content pedagogy standards, 53
Content validity, 10
Copy-protected graphics, 131
Copyright law, 126–127, 135
Council of Chief State School Officers (CCSSO), 58
Cropping, 173
Curriculum and Content Area Standards, 57
Curriculum knowledge, 62
Curry School Center for Technology and Teacher Education, 96
Custom Animation task pane, 123, 125

DAW, 190–191
Design templates, importing, 114
Dewey, John, 11, 13
Digital cameras, 172–173, 189
photography hints, 173–175
Digital Millennium Copyright Act (DMCA), 126
Digital video
cameras, 172–173, 189
capturing and using, 175–178
See also Video
Digital zoom, 173
Digitizers, 176
Disk, readability of, 192
Disk-at-once (DAO) recording, 182
Diverse learners reflection, 67

Diverse learners standards, 53*f*
DOS, 181
Dots per inch (dpi), 169, 171, 172
DVD
cost of, 184
DVD-R, 183, 184
DVD RAM, 183–184
DVD-RW, 183–184
saving information to, 179, 183–184
storage capacity of double-sided, 202

Easy Presentations, 104*t*
Educational Testing Service (ETS), 11
Effect Enhancements, 125
Effect Options, 125
Electronic Musician, 158
Elementary and Secondary Education Act (ESEA), 54
Elementary students, portfolio example, 38
Embedded files, 134
Entrance or Other Option, 125
E-portfolio
authoring tools, 95*t*
authoring tools, choosing, 106–107*t*
defining, 6
future of, 202–204
more effective, 202–204
non-Web-based tools, 100–104*t*
primary function of, 187
purpose of, 149, 161–162, 189
selecting portfolio tools, 104–106
Web-based tools, 94–100, 104*t*
See also PowerPoint
Epson Presenters Online, 78
Error patterns
guide to common errors, 191–194
top 10 list of, 197–198
Escape key, 120
Evaluation
defining, 6
standards for, 46
vs. assessment, 5–6

Excel, 181
Exit portfolio, 7, 49, 54
Expectations of Excellence: Curriculum Standards for Social Studies and *Standards for the Preparation of Social Studies Teachers*, 56–57

Fair use, 126–129
    amount of copyrighted work, 128
    market effects, 128
    nature of work, 127–128
    purpose/character of use, 127
Family partnerships standards, 55*f*
File conversion, 148–149
File extensions, 148*f*, 181, 193
File-name length, hyperlink, 136
Fill Color, 137
Firewire, 160
Five Core Propositions, 58
Flash drive, 173
Flatbed scanner, 170, 172
Floppy disk, 178–179
Font type and size, 116–117
Foreign language standards Web site, 56
Format pull-down menu, 117
From File, 129
Full pathway, hyperlink, 136

Gallery, 132
General pedagogical knowledge, 62
Goal setting, 6, 8, 71, 86–87, 88
    elementary student form, 87*f*
Goldwave, 158
Go to Slide option, 121
Grabe, C., 12
Grabe, M., 12
Graphic images, format for saving, 148*f*
Group Text, 125

Handout, printing, 138–139
Handout Master, 139
Harvard Graduate School of Education's Project on the Next Generation of Teachers, 84
Head shots, 174

Helvetica font, 118
Horton, Sarah, 79
Hyperlinks, 135–137, 144–147, 146*f*, 190–191
    action button for, 137
    action settings, 194
    creating on Web page, 201
    erasing, 200
    to reflections, 188
    relative, 180–181, 194
    troubleshooting, 194
HyperStudio, 100–102, 104*t*
HyperText Markup Language (HTML), 95–96
    saving presentation in, 198–201

IDVD, 183
IEEE 1394, 160, 176
ILink, 160
Image size, 153–154, 168–169
Images, nonlinear presentation
    color, contrast, and brightness, 156–157
    cropping, 150–153
    editing with Photoshop Elements, 149–159
    filtering, 154–156
    size adjustment, 153–154
Images of individuals, permission to use, 150, 151*f*–152*f*
IMovie, 148, 159, 176
Individuals, permission to use images of, 150, 151*f*–152*f*
Insert button, 116, 129
Insert pull-down menu, 129, 132, 133, 134, 135
Insert tab, 132, 135, 137
In-service teachers
    proficiency portfolios, 26
    progress-oriented portfolios, 25
    teaching portfolio, example, 33–35
Instructional format, 16–17
Instructional resources standards, 55*f*
Instructional strategies reflection, 67
INTASC (Interstate New Teacher Assessment and Support Consortium), 27–28, 47, 53*f*, 58

INTASC standards for beginning teachers, 12, 14, 53*f*
Intelligent action, 13
International Organization for Standardization (ISO), 181
International Reading Association (IRA), 56
International Technology Education Association (ITEA), 44, 58
ISO 9660 format, 181, 192
ISTE National Educational Technology Standards for Teachers (NETS•T), 45–46

Joliet, 181
JPEG images, 146, 148, 148*f*, 154, 168, 172, 173, 181
Jupitermedia Corporation, 78–79

Kardos, S. M., 84
Kendall, J., 44
Kennesaw State University, 96
Keynote (Apple), 100–101
KidPixs, 104*t*, 105
Knowledge categories, 62–63
Knowledge of subject matter standards, 55*f*
Knowledge of young adolescents standards, 55*f*

Language arts standards Web site, 56
Learning environment reflection, 68
Learning environment standards, 55*f*
Lesson effectiveness, evaluation criteria for, 63–66
Linear programs, 101
Literacy assessment, 15–16
Liu, E., 84
Local e-portfolio tools, 100–104*t*
Lynch, Patrick, 79

Mac OSX operating system, 109–110
animation, 125
Copy Image, 131
Edit pull-down menu, 131

file conversion, 148
hyperlinks, 137
iMovie, 148, 159
Internet graphics, adding, 131–132*f*
Paste Special, 131
PowerPoint linear presentation, 112
Save Image, 131
Save Target, 133
saving document files in, 167–168
slide transition, 125
sound, adding, 133
sound recorder, 132
starting PowerPoint, 119
Macromedia Cold Fusion, 104*t*
Macromedia Director, 104*t*
Martin, E., 23
Martin-Kniep, G., 14
Marzano, R., 44
Mathematics standards Web site, 56
Meaningful learning standards, 55*f*
Media, saving portfolio to
CD, 179–183
DVD, 179, 183–184
Media Player (Windows), 195, 197
Memory, 178
Memory card, 173, 175
Memory stick, 173, 175
Metacognition, defining, 7
Micromedia, 104*t*
Microsoft Front Page, 96
Microsoft Internet Explorer, 95
Microsoft Office, 100
MIDI (musical instrument digital interface), 133, 148*f*
Modern Language Association (MLA), 129
Monitor size, 168–169
Morton, J. L., 79
Motivation and management standards, 53*f*
Movies and Sound, 132, 133, 134
Moving PowerPoint presentation to Web, 198–202
MPEG (MPEG-1 Audio Layer-3), 148*f*, 176

MP3 files, 133, 148*f*, 193
MS Word
    file extensions, 181
    importing RTF file into, 166–167
Multiple documents, 44
Multiple instructional strategies
    standards, 53*f*
Multiple paths to knowledge
    standards, 55*f*
Music education standards, 57
Music format, compatibility with
    hardware, 138

Napster, 126
*National Arts Education
    Associations*, 57
National Association of State
    Directors of Teacher Education
    and Certification
    (NASDTEC), 12, 33
National Board certified teacher
    (NBCT), 54
National Board for Professional
    Teaching Standards (NBPTS),
    12, 33–35, 49, 55*f*, 58
National Commission on Excellence
    in Education, 11
National Council for Accreditation
    of Teacher Education
    (NCATE), 47
National Council for the Social
    Studies (NCSS), 44
National Council of Teachers of
    English (NCTE), 44, 56
National Council of Teachers of
    Mathematics (NCTM), 44
National Educational Technology
    Standards for Teachers
    (NETS•T), 45–46
National Education Technology
    Standards (NETS), 57
*National Science Education
    Standards*, 56
National Science Teachers
    Association (NSTA), 44
National Standards for Arts
    Education, 57

A Nation at Risk, 11
Netscape, 104*t*
Netscape Composer, 96
Netscape Navigator, 95
New Presentation, 114
New Slide, 116
New Teacher Assessment and
    Support Consortium
    (INTASC), 188
No Child Left Behind Act
    (NCLB), 54
The Non-designers Web Book
    (Williams & Tollet), 79
Non–Web-based (local)
    e-portfolio tools
    advanced features, 101–103
    Apple Keynote, 104*t*
    Easy Presentations, 104*t*
    hyperlinking, 101–102
    HyperStudio, 104*t*
    KidPixs, 104*t*, 105
    Micromedia Director, 104*t*
    MS PowerPoint, 104*t*
    Open Office Impress, 104*t*
    selected authoring
        systems, 103, 104*t*
    Word Perfect Presentations, 104*t*
Normal view, 118–119
Notes view, 120

Office 2003 (Microsoft), 109
Office 2007 (Microsoft), 109
Opening files, troubleshooting, 193
Open Office Impress, 94, 104*t*
Optical zoom, 173
Other Option, 125
*Outcomes of Quality Physical
    Education*, 57

Paper-and-pencil portfolio, 189
Password protection, 149
Pathway, hyperlink, 136
Pedagogical content knowledge, 62
Penn State University, 96
Pennsylvania Department of
    Education (PDE), 49, 54
Performance assessment, 7

Performance-based learning, 7
Performance standards, 7
Photographs, 35, 37, 189
   hints for digital, 173–175
Physical education standards
      Web site, 57
Piaget, J., 11–12
Pixels, 168–169
Plagiarism, 129
Planning portfolios, 26–28, 188–191
Planning/designing learning
      environments/experiences
      standards, 45–46
Planning instruction reflection, 68
Planning standards, 53f
Play CD Audio Track
      dialog box, 134
Pointer option, 121
Portfolio
   authentic tasks for, 4–5
   defining, 3–4
   electronic vs. traditional, 4
   power of, 14–15
   purpose of, 22
   uses of, 4
   See also Portfolio development
Portfolio development
   assessment, advantages of, 7, 8–9
   assessment, disadvantages
      of, 9–11
   introduction, 3–5
   performance-based
      movement, 11–12
   planning for, 26–28
   reflection as integral to, 13–14
   scenario example, 15–18
   terms used in, 5–8
   Web sites for, 56–58
Portfolio name, troubleshooting, 194
Portfolio Party, 86
Portrait shots, 174
PowerPoint, 78, 94, 100–101, 104t
   advantages of, 106–107
   presentation overview, 190–191
   selecting slide background, 114
   sequence for creating basic
      presentation, 118f

troubleshooting, 191–194, 207–208
   See also PowerPoint 2007;
      PowerPoint, linear
      presentation; PowerPoint,
      nonlinear presentation
PowerPoint 2007
   animation, 125
   clip art, adding, 130
   font adjustments, 116
   Go to Slide option, 121
   Handout Master, 139
   hyperlink, adding, 137
   initiating operations, 119
   Insert tab, 132, 135, 137
   movies, adding, 135
   opening preexisting file, 112
   pictures, adding, 130
   Pointer option, 121
   saving files in, 113
   saving presentations in, 181
   slide backgrounds, 115
   Slide Show tab, 121
   slide transition, 125
   sound, adding, 135
   video clips, adding, 135
   View tab, 121
PowerPoint, linear presentation
   Action Button, 137
   Action Settings, 137
   Add Effect, 125
   advantages of, 142–143, 190
   animation, 123–125, 124f
   auto-content wizard, 114
   bulleted lists, 116, 123
   Category, 129
   Clip Art, 129
   clip art, adding, 129–130
   clip art, resizing, 130
   Custom Animation task
      pane, 123, 125
   default view, 113
   design templates, importing, 114
   diagram of, 101, 102f
   editing slide, 121
   Effect Enhancements, 125
   Effect Options, 125
   Entrance or Other Option, 125

escape key, 120
fair use (*See* Fair use)
From File, 129
Fill Color, 137
font type and size, 116–117
Format pull-down menu, 117
Gallery, 132
Getting Started, 114
graphics, 123
Group Text, 125
handout printing, 138–139
Insert button, 116, 129
Insert pull-down menu, 129, 132,
    133, 134, 135
Internet images, adding, 130–132*f*
Internet or document links,
    adding, 135–137
limitations, 142, 143
mapping project, 110
movies, adding, 134–135
Movies and Sound, 132, 133, 134
music, adding, 123
navigation tools, 121
New Presentation, 114
New Slide, 116
Normal view, 118–119
Notes view, 120
ordering slides, 119
outline for planning, 110
Picture, 129
Play CD Audio Track
    dialog box, 134
Record Sound, 133
Save Image to File, 131
sequence for adding slide
    transition/animation, 124*f*
showing presentation, 138–139
slide background, selecting,
    113–116
Slide Design, 114
slide icon, 121
Slide Show command, 121
Slide Show pull-down menu,
    122, 123, 137
Slide Show view, 120
Slide Sorter view, 119
Slide Template, 116

Slide Transition, 122–123
Slide View, 120–121
sound, adding, 132–134
sound, adding from CD, 134
speaking notes, 120
special effects, 122–123
starting PowerPoint, 111–113
stopping slide show, 120
storyboard approach, 110, 143
Text Animation tab, 125
Text Box, 135
title/subtitle of presentation, 112
View menu, 118–119
View pull-down menu, 117
View Show, 138
See also PowerPoint,
    nonlinear presentation
PowerPoint, nonlinear presentation
artifact files, 146
e-portfolio, building, 147–149
e-portfolio, collecting/digitizing
    artifacts, 147–148
e-portfolio, planning, 147
file conversion, 148–149
hyperlinking, 144–147, 146*f*
hyperlinking, external, 144–145
hyperlinking, internal, 144
images, color, contrast, and
    brightness, 156–157
images, cropping, 150–153
images, editing with Photoshop
    Elements, 149–159
images, filtering, 154–156
images, size adjustment,
    153–154
indexes, 147
nondocument artifact files, format
    for saving, 148*f*
order of slides, 144–145
questionable content, 159
sound, editing, 157–159
video, editing, 159–162
See also PowerPoint,
    linear presentation
PowerPoint reader, downloading,
    194–195
PowerPoint Viewer, 195

Presentation tools, non-Web-based
    e-portfolio, 100–104*t*
Presenting portfolios
  alignment, 79
  color, 77, 79
  font size and type, 76–77
  to others, 79–80
  professional development
      presentations, 88
  proximity, 79
  quality contrast, 79
  repetition, 79
  resources for design decisions,
      78–79
  skills, 76–78
  student portfolios, 85–88
  See also Presenting teacher
      portfolios
Presenting teacher
    portfolios, 80–85
  exit portfolio presentation, 80–81
  interview presentations, 81, 84–85
  scoring rubric, 82*f*–83*f*
Preservice teachers
  communication portfolio,
      example, 30
  learning environment portfolio,
      example, 29–30
  proficiency portfolios, 26
  progress-oriented portfolios, 25
  purpose of portfolio, 46–47
  reflection and, 17
  University of Scranton Unit Exit
      Standards, example, 30
*Principles and Standards for School
    Mathematics*, 56
Problem-solving pedagogy, 17–18
Productivity and professional
    practice standards, 46
Product-oriented proficiency
    portfolio, 24
Professional development
    reflection, 69
Professional portfolio, 23–24
Proficiency portfolios, 22, 25–26
  for teachers, 28–35
Progress-oriented portfolios, 24, 25

QuickTime, downloading, 195, 197
QuickTime PictureViewer, 148
QuickTime Player, 148

Readable font, 117
Reflection
  defining, 7, 13
  hyperlinks to, 188
  as integral to portfolio
      development, 13–14
  preservice teacher, 17
  professional growth and, 53*f*
  self-assessment and, 63
Reflective practice standards, 55*f*
Relative hyperlinks, 136, 180–181
Reliability, 9, 10
Report card conference,
    student/parent/teacher, 86
Resources for standards, Web sites,
    56–58
Respect for diversity standards, 55*f*
RGB (red, green, and blue), 168
Ross, D., 62
RTF (rich text) file, importing into
    MS Word, 166–167
Rubrics
  defining, 7, 63
  research strategies, 72*f*
  scoring, 82*f*–83*f*
  self-assessment, 63–65, 70*f*

Save As command (File menu), 112,
    113, 148, 154, 166, 167, 199
Save As File Type window,
    166, 199, 201
Save As pop-up box, 201
Save Image to File, 131
Saving
  audio, 148*f*
  CD burning, 179–183
  DVD, saving information to,
      179, 183–184
  graphic images, 148*f*
  in HTML, 198–201
  in Macintosh platform, 131, 133,
      167–168
  nondocument artifact files, 148*f*

in PowerPoint 2007, 113, 181
troubleshooting, 191–192, 193
video, 148*f*
in Windows platform,
    166–167, 168
Scanners, 168, 170–172, 189
Schön, Donald, 13
School and community
    development standards, 53*f*
Science standards Web site, 56
Secondary student portfolio,
    example, 39, 41, 42*f*
Seldin, Peter, 26–27
Self-assessment, 4
    defining, 8, 61
    process of, 66
    reflection and, 63
    rubrics for, 63–65
    See also Self-assessment, for
        students; Self-assessment,
        for teachers
Self-assessment, for students, 70–73
    plant journal rubric, 70*f*
    questions to prompt, 71
    research strategies rubric, 72*f*
Self-assessment, for teachers, 66–69
    assessment, 68
    collaboration, ethics, and
        relationships, 68–69
    communication, 68
    diverse learners, 67
    instructional strategies, 67
    learning environment, 68
    planning instruction, 68
    professional development, 69
    sample questions for, 66–67, 69
    student learning, 67
    subject matter, 67
Shareware, 149–150, 157–158, 163
Sheet-fed scanner, 170, 172
Shulman, Lee, 62–63
Slide Show pull-down menu,
    122, 123, 137, 200
Slides
    Mac OSX operating system, 125
    ordering in PowerPoint nonlinear
        presentation, 144–145

troubleshooting transitions,
    192–193
See also Slides, PowerPoint 2007;
    Slides, PowerPoint linear
    presentation
Slides, PowerPoint 2007
    background, 115
    Slide Show tab, 121
    slide transition, 125
Slides, PowerPoint linear
    presentation
    background, 113–116
    Slide Design, 114, 116
    slide icon, 121
    slide show, stopping, 120
    Slide Show command, 121
    Slide Show pull-down menu,
        122, 123, 137
    Slide Show view, 120
    Slide Sorter view, 119
    Slide Template, 116
    Slide Transition, 122–123
    Slide View, 120–121
Social, ethical, legal, and human
    issues standards, 46
Social development standards, 55*f*
Social studies standards
    Web site, 56–57
Sound, 125
    capturing, 133
    format for saving, 148*f*
    linear presentation, 132, 133, 134
    nonlinear presentation, editing,
        157–159
    WAVE files, 193
    WAV files, 133
    See also Sound, adding
Sound, adding
    from CD, 134
    Mac OSX operating system, 133
    PowerPoint, 132
    PowerPoint 2007, 135
Sound files, memory needs, 162
Sound recorder
    in Macintosh platform, 132
    in Windows platform, 132, 133
Standardized testing, 10–11

Standards
  assessment, 46, 53*f*, 55*f*
  development by individual states, 45
  evaluation, 46
  INTASC standards for beginning
    teachers, 12, 14, 53*f*
  language arts Web site, 56
  learning environment, 55*f*
  mathematics Web site, 56
  NBPTS, 55*f*
  performance, 7
  technology, 45–46, 53*f*, 57
Standards for fine arts, 57
*Standards for Foreign Language
  Learning in the 21st Century,* 56
Standard XII, NBPTS, 35, 36*f*
Student development standards, 53*f*
Student learning reflection, 67
Student/parent/teacher report card
  conference, 86
Student portfolios, 39, 41, 42*f*, 85–88
Students, empowering, 86
Student-teacher conference, 71
Subject matter reflection, 67

Talking standards for beginning
  teachers, 58
TaskStream, 98, 104*t*
Task System, 104*t*
Teaching, learning, and curriculum
  standards, 46
Teaching philosophy, example, 32
Teaching portfolio for rank and
  tenure in higher education,
  example, 31–33, 34*f*
Teaching standards for
  beginning/veteran teachers, 58
Technological Literacy Standards, 5
Technology
  standards, 45–46, 53*f*, 57
  USB, 159–160, 173, 176
Technology Education and
  Copyright Harmonization
  (TEACH) Act, 126, 159
*Technology Foundation Standards for
  All Students,* 57
Technology skills, 37

Text Animation tab, 125
Text Box, 135
Theme IX, NCSS, 41
Times New Roman font, 117–118
Tollet, J., 79
Trigwell, K., 23
Troubleshooting, PowerPoint-based
  e-portfolio, 191–194, 207–208

University of Scranton
  alignment with INTASC
    standards, 51*f*–52*f*
  on preservice teachers,
    47, 48*f*, 50*f*–52*f*
  sampling of artifacts using
    Scranton model, 50*f*
University of Wisconsin at La
  Crosse (UW-L), 96
USB technology, 159–160, 173, 176

VHS, 189
Video, 6, 35, 77–78
  adding to PowerPoint 2007, 135
  capturing and using digital,
    175–178
  compatibility with
    hardware, 138
  editing, 160–161
  format for saving, 148*f*
  hyperlinks to, 146, 161
  importing, 159–160
  memory needs, 162
VideoStudio 7, 158
View menu, 118–119
View pull-down menu, 117
View Show, 138
View tab, 121
Vista operating system, 109–110
Voiceover, 14

WAVE sound files, 193
WAV (waveform sound for
  Microsoft Windows), 133, 148*f*
Web-based e-portfolios
  authoring tools, 104*t*
  media for, 100
  memory allotment, 98–99

navigation tools, 99
nonlinear pathways
    available in, 97*f*
strengths/weaknesses
    of, 99–100
templates, 98, 99
Web Style Guide, 79
Williams, R., 76, 79
Windows Media Player, 195, 197
Windows Movie Maker, 159

Windows platform
    saving document files in,
        166–167, 168
    sound recorder in, 132, 133
Windows XP (Microsoft), 110
WordPerfect Presentations, 94, 104*t*
Working portfolio, 22

Zoom feature, digital camera, 173
Zubizarreta, J., 31–32

About the Authors

Kathleen Montgomery is an Associate Professor in the Education Department at the University of Scranton. She is an elementary education generalist who has taught Grades K–8 for 16 years in the United States as well as in international schools. She served as the Director of Undergraduate and Graduate Programs at the University of Scranton and has authored numerous articles and a book on alternative assessment methods, including portfolio assessment.

David A. Wiley is a Professor in the Education Department at the University of Scranton in Scranton, Pennsylvania. After teaching science for more than 14 years, he moved to the university in 1988. He has served as Department Chair for over 9 years, is now serving as Certification Officer, and was a coauthor of the assessment plan used with teacher candidates at the University of Scranton. His research interests include mathematics and science education, technology education, and teacher effectiveness in the classroom setting. He has authored articles and books in his areas of expertise, and he has presented at the Pennsylvania and the National Science Teachers Associations, the American Association of Colleges of Teacher Education, and meetings of many other organizations. His service agenda is heavy in the area of teacher preparation and working with science teacher professional associations.